Praise for *Where Have I Been All My Life?*

"Any woman raised on a diet of people-pleasing, and fairy-tale-believing will adore Rice's memoir."

—**CAROLINE ADAMS MILLER,** author of *Creating Your Best Life, My Name is Caroline,* and *Positively Caroline*

"A very powerful, moving journey of a woman who eloquently bears her soul with extraordinary candor both as a child, mother, wife, and successful career woman in a way that is truly inspirational."

—**JUDITH VON SELDENECK,** Chairman and CEO, Diversified Search

"If you've known for a long time that you need to open the door on the past in order to find your hopeful future, this book is for you. With tenderness, candor, and unflinching honesty, Rice shows us how to examine our lives at those key moments when being in the dark is the only way to safely find our way home again. A perfect companion during times of transition, loss, or self-discovery, *Where Have I Been All My Life?* offers a narrative of curiosity and courage that will inspire any woman at a crossroads, trying to make sense of her wild and precious life."

—**JEN LEMEN,** co-founder of Hopeful World

"*Where Have I Been All My Life?* is a beautifully written and courageous story told with grace, humor, and grit. Anyone interested in living a life of authenticity and self-compassion will greatly benefit from reading this compelling book."

—**MIKE ROBBINS,** *author of Nothing Changes Until You Do*

"Where Have I Been All My Life? vividly describes what is not often disclosed in books about grief: how losing one's mother can cause a woman to question everything about her life and herself. In the journey that is this book, Rice confronts her longings for the unattainable, her compulsion to take care of everyone else— even her therapist—and her inability to fully accept herself. From the very first page, I could relate. I know the longing and the self-loathing Rice writes of all too well, and I suspect many other women do too. With humor and grace, and through the process of crafting this poignant and humane book, Rice accepts loss, recognizes the impossibility of long-held fantasies, and is able to finally take in real love."

—**DEBORAH A. LOTT,** author of *In Session: The Bond Between Women and Their Therapists* and *Don't Go Crazy Without Me*

"Rice's book captures the essence of looking outside for affirmation, for approval, for acceptance. Her journey is a familiar one for women. Until we love ourselves, there is never enough. It's an inside job, and her story will help other women tell their stories as well."

—**MARSHA CLARK,** Founder, Marsha Clark & Associates

"Cheryl Rice is a fantastic writer. I was completely engaged from page one. I love her work and you will too."

—**NANCY SLONIM ARONIE,** author of *Writing From the Heart: Tapping the Power of Your Inner Voice*

"*Where Have I Been All My Life?* is a powerfully compelling memoir. Any woman who aspires to be a leader in her own life will value this heartfelt book."

—**SALLY STETSON**, Principal, Salveson Stetson Group

"In her moving memoir, *Where Have I Been All My Life?*, Rice offers a tender and generous voice to the personal struggle for worthiness— an issue that most professional women grapple with but few dare discuss."

—**JENNIFER A. CHAMBERS**, MD, MBA, FACP, Chief Medical Officer, Capital Blue Cross

"*Where Have I Been All My Life?* is a powerful memoir that will be meaningful to anyone who has experienced the deep loss of a loved one. We are comforted and inspired by Rice's journey from grief to inner strength, love and wholeness. "

—**MICHELE W. DALY**, Executive Director, Women's Resource Center

"*Where Have I Been All My Life?* is a source of hope and courage for anyone willing to honestly look inside him or herself to discover a more fulfilling life. Rice bares it all to give us a model of what it takes to acknowledge the psychological complexes driving our behavior and forgive the parents who unknowingly planted them there."

—**MICHAEL NAGLE**, Owner, Michael Nagle Consulting Group

WHERE HAVE I BEEN
ALL MY LIFE?

WHERE HAVE I BEEN ALL MY LIFE?

A JOURNEY TOWARD LOVE
AND WHOLENESS

CHERYL RICE

SHE WRITES PRESS

Published 2014
Printed in the United States of America
ISBN: 978-1-63152-917-7
Library of Congress Control Number: 2014936411

Permission for opening quote by Terri St. Cloud
of Bone Sigh Arts; www.bonesigharts.com

For information, address:
She Writes Press
1563 Solano Ave #546
Berkeley, CA 94707

For
Mom and Dad

She could never go back and make
some of the details pretty.
All she could do was move forward
and make the whole beautiful.

—Terri St. Cloud

CONTENTS

PREFACE

I entered the hospital room where my mother was being treated for pneumonia and dehydration—side effects of the aggressive doses of chemotherapy and radiation she was enduring to squelch the stage IV lung cancer that had been found two months earlier. She was just sixty-seven years old. I was the self-appointed quarterback of her care team and made it my priority to be physically and emotionally present for her every day of the six precious months between her diagnosis and her death.

Back in the hospital room, before I could even ask how she was feeling, Mom propped herself up on her pillow, looked straight into my eyes, and said, "Well, honey, now you can write your book."

I was stunned. Though Mom knew of my long-buried dream of writing a book one day, she also knew the dream was tamped down tightly by paralyzing fears and doubts that I had anything worthwhile to say. I couldn't recall the last time we had discussed it.

"What would my book be about, Mom?" I asked, genuinely curious.

"How to help your mother die."

Well, I wrote a book. But it's not about helping my mother die. It's about helping myself live. It's about how losing my best friend, the person whose voice I trusted most in this world, called me forth to befriend myself and claim my own voice in deep, unprecedented, and vital ways. And it's about learning to exchange a fantasy life, fueled by a stark fear of intimacy, for a real life fueled by the vulnerability and messiness of real love.

I was forty-five years old. I had a three-years-new marriage to a handsome, charming, kind-hearted man with two wonderful children whom I was privileged to help raise. I had a vibrant career as a leadership and life coach. I had my mom and dad living close by—accomplished and wonderful people I cherished, respected, and in many ways idolized. Aside from the chaos our new puppy caused, my life looked quite stable and very good. I told myself I was blessed despite nagging feelings to the contrary.

Then grief blew up the glimmering patina of the perfect life that I had cultivated. It brought me to a frightening, uncomfortable, and unfamiliar world where I had no sense of direction or compass to tell me where to go next. Finding my way through this unfamiliar terrain required wrestling and reconciling deeply held notions about myself and others—notions I considered sacrosanct.

Notions about me: my people-pleasing-at-all-costs ways; my investment in being seen as a good girl, a kind girl, a thin girl, a perfect girl, but not a real girl; and my unrelenting belief that my worthiness had to be earned—all the time.

Long-unchallenged notions about men and intimacy: I was masterful at giving love but often unable to receive it. I was convinced that wholeness and healing would come from outside me. And I used longing and the fantasies it fueled as an escape from pain and loneliness and ultimately as a poor substitute for real and available love.

Notions about my parents: My loyalty and love for them prevented me from seeing them as whole, humanly imperfect people. And I used that loyalty, and their general wonderfulness, to protect myself from acknowledging the full impact and pain some of their behavior caused me.

Challenging and in some cases letting go of these notions was not easy. It was a dizzying, often painful process. I fought tooth and nail, and I tried many clever tactics to avoid doing my work—the work of moving from childhood to adulthood.

For the past ten years, I have facilitated Women's Coaching Circles. Women come to the circle, often not knowing each other but having been moved by a flyer or an email or a friend of a friend who mentioned its being worthwhile. The purpose of the Coaching Circle is to provide a safe place for women to give voice to their dreams, their questions, their hopes and fears. I have come to believe that on some level each of the women who attends is looking for permission to be her authentic self, to take herself seriously, to trust her desires as valid, and to learn to listen to herself with abiding compassion and curiosity. Often, when a group member has just shared something deeply honest and is feeling understandably vulnerable, I will thank her for her courage and remind the group that she has really spoken for all of us. And unfailingly the other women in the circle nod their heads yes.

I hope that you will find a bit of yourself in these interweaving essays, that they will take you deeper into your own life experiences and provide some sustenance for the difficult yet vital journey toward love and wholeness—a journey we all must take if we want to be free. I hope they may, in some small way, lead you home.

HOMESICK

I don't remember saying good-bye. I must have blocked it out of my memory. I do remember my eleven-year-old thighs sticking to the vinyl seat of the sweltering silver charter bus. And I remember tears flowing steadily down my cheeks, my body barking out sobs, betraying my efforts to silently swallow them whole, and the final indignity: the stream of snot pouring from my nose.

I was despondent, and the bus hadn't even left the parking lot yet. Even my nine-year-old brother, Mark, pretended not to know me—and I couldn't blame him.

I had lost the most recent round of pleading with my parents not to send me to Camp Netimus, an all-girls camp two and a half hours north of home. Mark was attending an all-boys camp fifteen miles from mine.

"I'm not ready. I'll be good, I'll be better, I'm sorry for whatever I did wrong. Just don't send me away. Please."

"No. This is good for you. This will help you in the long run. Be a big girl. Your brother is already making friends. You'll be fine. Do you know how lucky you are?"

No. I didn't know how lucky I was. All I knew was that I was scared, and overwhelmed, and couldn't for the life of me figure out what I had done to cause this banishment.

My tears ebbed and flowed throughout the bus ride and resumed in earnest once I stepped into my assigned cabin. One of my counselors, Jackie, an eight-year camp veteran, tried—in vain—to comfort me, but after I had sniveled through the three packs of Kleenex my mother had packed in the top tray of my navy blue trunk, Jackie knew she was overmatched and ushered me to the infirmary.

At sleep-away camp, homesickness is treated like lice— something that must be immediately contained and treated, lest it spread throughout the cabin or, heaven forbid, the entire camp.

The infirmary nurse, I think her name was Olivia, was an evangelical Christian from Australia. And though I was Jewish, and she was clearly more accustomed to healing scrapes and sprains than wounded egos, I found comfort in her assurance that I was not alone and that Jesus was with me. In retrospect, telling my mother about Olivia's proselytizing may have been the one thing to have convinced her to retrieve me immediately— but I was too forlorn to think of it then.

For many kids, going to overnight camp at age eleven is no big deal. What could be more fun than an eight-week sleepover with one's best buddies? But, unfortunately, to me, eight weeks away from home felt impossible and unsurvivable, which is why my parents sent me to begin with.

One of my earliest memories is clinging to my mother's pant leg as we hobbled into my kindergarten class. Each school day began with my whimpering in front of my storage cubby, longing to join the girls and boys who were playing with puzzles and Play-Doh, but not feeling secure enough to join in. The teacher would eventually lose her cool and tell me how unhappy I was making my classmates. The only good moments came on the days my mother and I went to the school early so Mom could talk with the teacher. With Mom safely within reach, I was able to play in the toy kitchen, albeit alone. Not surprisingly, after a few miserable months of daily bawling, I was asked to withdraw from kindergarten and try again the following year.

Sleepovers proved equally agonizing. When I went to Debbie Pomeroso's house across the street, I perched myself in front of Debbie's bedroom window and peered out at my house, counting the hours until I could return, instead of counting sheep so I could sleep.

I don't know where separation anxiety like that comes from. I do know that Mom nicknamed me Poppet, which in her home country of South Africa means "doll" in Afrikaans. And that is what I was for her—not *a* doll, but *her* doll. The doll she clung to in social situations she was uncomfortable navigating alone in this country. The doll she needed to provide purpose and companionship when my father and her parents and friends were unavailable. And the doll I dutifully tried to be.

Throughout that first summer at camp, when other kids perfected the skills of canoeing or dance, I perfected the art of homesickness. It became routine to wake up and begin my day in tears even as I made my bed and raced to line up in front of the flagpole for reveille.

The counselors must have drawn straws to decide who would be on "homesick duty" with me each day. The unlucky winner would begin her day by sitting knee to knee with me on the steps to my cabin. Before the counselor could say a word, I'd apologize for my sadness and for keeping her from the "fun" kids. Then the counselor would list all the activities I could try and promise that the summer would go faster if I made friends, instead of making plans to leave. But I would have none of it and insisted that, as lovely a place as this was, my mom needed me and I wanted to go home. Next came the tears, and through my sobs I'd console the helpless counselor. "I'm so sorry," I would offer. "You don't have to sit with me. I'll be fine. I know being away from home is good for me in some way." Though, truthfully, I had no idea what that way was, but I felt compelled to give my parents the benefit of the doubt. Anything else would have been unimaginable.

Every day at rest hour, I would write my parents letters begging them to take me home. I found one of those letters when going through a box of papers Mom had stored in her attic.

Dear Mommy and Daddy,

I know you want me to have a good summer But I hate it here.

I've really tried hard.

You don't understand. The food is inedible *terrible.*

I feel so sick. Please take me home. I will be good forever. I don't like the people in my cabin they never talk to me. I'm running out of tissues so I'll have to come home to get some more.

Mom, this is my summer so let me do what i want.

Why are you sending me away—don't you love me. I'll run away next week.

Please, please, please take me home!!

Love,
Cheryl
P.S. 2 months is 2 long

I lulled myself to sleep imagining how shocked they would be if I actually did go AWOL. And when I wasn't planning my escape or writing pleading postcards, I silently prayed, to the Jesus Olivia had introduced me to, for my parents to take me home after four weeks instead of eight.

But my prayers and letter-writing campaign proved futile. One day my favorite counselor, Laura, escorted me into the camp office so the camp director, Betsy, could tell me my parents felt it was in my best interest to stay the full session. They wouldn't even tell me themselves. I can still smell the mix of cigarette smoke and coffee on Betsy's cotton Camp Netimus T-shirt as I wept inconsolably in her arms. She must have wanted to weep too, at the reality of another four weeks of this routine. Why, I wondered, why couldn't I spend the time helping my mom around the house, maybe go with her to the beach she loved so much and make lemonade with her instead of eating powdered eggs here at camp?

Ironically, at the end of that summer I was given the camp's most celebrated award, the Camp Life Award. I was the youngest camper ever to receive it at the time. I'm quite sure the counselors gave it to me because they were shocked I had actually survived.

I went on to spend ten summers at camp: six as a camper and four as a counselor. Even the last few years, when I went to camp willingly, I began each season in tears the way most kids begin it by claiming the top bunk. And I developed an exquisite talent for moving away from my own feelings in order to survive, an accomplishment for which there was no award.

Not surprisingly, one of my specialties was counseling homesick campers and their parents. Another was riflery. I would lie down on a wooden platform lined with stained and musty mattresses, load a rifle half as tall as I was, aim straight ahead, and pull the trigger. (I can still recall the metallic smell from the casings that spilled from the gun after I fired it.) Then, though we were supposed to walk, I would run to retrieve my target and add up my score. I was so accurate, the head of the riflery department regularly sent me to other camps to compete. Funny that of all the camp activities for me to excel at, riflery was the one. Perhaps it was the only acceptable way to discharge my frustration at the time.

Of course, there were many wonderful takeaways from my time at camp: friends from all over the world; camp songs I still sing in the shower; Tuesday-night dances with boys from our brother camp (the cuter the guy, the less likely he was to dance and the more quickly I averted my eyes when he, or any boy, even accidently looked my way); and an enduring affection for the smell of trees, campfires, and dewed grass.

But the good doesn't balance out the bad. It sits beside it.

And for me, the bad stuff was stickier. I believed I was sent to camp because I wasn't good enough or worthy enough to stay with my parents. Somehow I had failed them, and this was my punishment. I couldn't appreciate their desire to teach me independence— I was too bereft. Homesickness became my defining life arc. Longing to be somewhere else and feel something else became habitual. Enduring *now* for a far-off *then* became my sustaining talent.

When I was at camp, I yearned to be home with Mom. When I was home, I yearned for a boy and later a man who would rescue me from my loneliness. When I was fat, I yearned to be thin. And when I got thin, I yearned to be thinner. When I grew up and went on vacations, I yearned to be home and invariably found reasons to return early (convinced my cats and dog needed me as much as I needed them). And when I finally found that man, I yearned for him to fit my ideal of marriage. When I lost my mom, I yearned for her again.

But what I yearned for most, what I was most homesick for, was a welcoming, sheltering, and abiding home within. Learning to cultivate that abiding sense of self would come to be my most worthwhile journey of all.

And the journey began the moment my mother died.

APRIL FOOLS' DAY

It was an unusually warm and cloudless spring day, the kind of day when it finally feels safe to put away wool sweaters and begin thinking about what kind of vegetables to plant in the garden. It was also April 1—a day for harmless pranks and sanctioned silliness. But for me, there was nothing sunny or silly happening.

The evening before, following my family's instructions to contact us immediately if my mother's condition took a turn for the worse, the night nurse called me at 1:00 AM, saying she thought Mom was dying. I had taken to sleeping in yoga pants and a T-shirt so I could leave the house quickly in case this call arrived at night. I told Alan, my husband, that "this could be it," and to feed and walk our dog, Gracie, if I wasn't home by morning. Then I jumped in my car and spent the entire thirty-minute drive praying I would arrive in time to say my last good-bye.

I ran into Mom's room and found my father and aunt at her bedside. I could tell from their grave expressions that Mom was still alive. My aunt stepped away, and I immediately went to Mom's side and kissed her cheek.

"It's me, Mom. Cheryl. I love you and I'm here."

Though her eyes were closed, as they had been for the past week, we had been told she could likely still hear us. Her cheeks, so often filled with crimson, were now a chalky gray. Her breathing was deep, and despite the rose-scented lip balm we often applied, her lips were stiff and cracked.

We took turns whispering gently to Mom. I told her how proud I was to be her daughter, how she was always there for me, and how I would always be here for her. I thanked her for being an extraordinary mom and my best friend. I tried desperately not to cry.

An hour later, the nurse checked Mom's vital signs and assured us she had stabilized. She didn't think she would die that night after all and suggested we go home and get some rest. Before I left, I took Mom's hand in mine, closed my eyes, and willed myself to memorize the warm and tender feel of her skin.

"Mom, we're going to go home and get some sleep. I'll be back in a few hours. But if you need to go and I'm not here, it's okay, Mom—you go. You can float away when you're ready." ("Floating" was the word Mom and I came up with to help her relax during chemo and radiation. She would close her eyes and imagine herself adrift in her beloved sea.) "I'll take care of Dad, don't worry. And, Mom, I'll be fine too. Be at peace."

Peaceful was the last thing I felt as I climbed back into bed, agonizing about what Mom was experiencing. Was she scared? Was she upset we had left her? Was she in pain? Or was she already gone, her brain and body beyond reach—certainly beyond repair? I wanted to stay awake in case I felt a shiver up my spine or a stab of pain in my heart if she did float away. But I didn't really believe she would go on her own. Mom had made it clear she

wanted us with her when she died. She was ever the perfect or-
ganizer, so I couldn't imagine something as vital as her death not
going according to her plan. Then again, I couldn't have imagined cancer taking hold of her and mercilessly destroying her
joyful, purposeful, and otherwise healthy self in just six months.

The next day, I woke up at 6:00 AM, determined to get to the
nursing home as early as possible. When I arrived, I could see by
the weighted look on the nurse's face that things were not good.
She quietly but assuredly said that Mom was now in the "active
dying" phase of death, and that I should call my father and aunt
right away.

It was a Thursday, which meant that my father was at
school, at the first of two college classes he had taught for the
past forty years. In all those years, even during Mom's illness, he
had never missed a single lecture.

Because he didn't carry a cell phone, Dad and I had agreed
that I would call campus security if I needed to reach him in an
emergency. Trembling, I pulled the telephone number from my
wallet. When I told the security officer what was happening, he
assured me someone would go to my father's classroom immediately and tell him he was needed at the nursing home right
away. Then I called my aunt, who was just about to leave her
house to come, her sisterly sense telling her the time was near.

I perched on Mom's bed and started stroking her hand and
caressing her cheek. "I'm here, Mom. Dad and Aunt Sandy are on
their way. I love you, Mom. I love you so much."

I silently prayed Dad would arrive safely before she died.
It was now rush hour in Philadelphia, and I knew he would be
virtually out of his mind driving twelve miles from the university
to the nursing home, hoping to make it in time.

Moments later, my aunt arrived and began speaking softly to Mom and stroking her other hand and cheek. For a while I timed my breaths to match Mom's, wanting to keep her company as long as I could, wanting to stay in sync, wanting perhaps to breathe life back into her—to breathe for both of us. But soon her breaths became less frequent and I found I couldn't hold my own back any longer—I had to breathe for myself.

At one point, some spit-up poured from Mom's mouth and I ran to the nurses' station to get Natalie, her favorite nurse. The last thing I wanted was for Mom's last moments to be a struggle. Natalie ran to Mom's room and swiftly cleared her mouth and throat. Then she checked the monitor next to the bed and quietly began to cry.

About fifteen minutes later, my father bounded into the room. Wordlessly relieved, I moved down on my side of Mom's bed so Dad could be by her face. He bent down, whispered in her ear, and gently kissed her lips. Not a moment later, Mom exhaled for the last time and died. I have no doubt that she saved her last breath for him.

Numbly, I moved to the terrace outside Mom's room and called my brother in Georgia, Alan, and my mom's best friend. The sun was already warm, but I was shivering and pacing as I spoke.

While we waited for the staff from the crematory to arrive, I awkwardly moved about, not knowing quite where to stand, since being next to Mom's cooling body felt slightly morbid, yet not being next to her, as I had been for the past six months, felt horribly wrong too.

But I had to keep moving. If I kept moving, maybe I could keep the truth from finding me. If I kept moving, maybe I could add value and not have to consider that the most valuable person in my life had just left this room, this planet, my life. If I kept moving, maybe God would see how much I still needed her, what a good daughter I was, and bring her back immediately. Maybe, just maybe, if I kept moving, Mom would sit up and ask us to forgive this most tasteless of April Fools' Day jokes.

Hurriedly, I began packing up her room. I gave the baskets of pansies and unopened boxes of crackers to the nurses and other staff members, knowing it would make Mom happy. I placed the CD player and classical music in a box, though I doubted I'd ever be able to listen to it again. Then I collected the tapestry of cards that lined her dresser and walls and gently added them to the already-full shoebox of well wishes that we kept by Mom's bed. I had to fight the urge not to read a few of them out loud to her, even now.

When the men from the crematory arrived, my aunt told me not to watch and guided me outside the room. As I walked out, I handed the men the box of cards Mom wanted cremated with her and reflexively reminded them to be gentle with her— she had endured enough already.

Once her body was gone and the room was returned to its original, sterile state, I asked Dad if he wanted me to come to their home and stay with him awhile. He said he would rather be alone, so I hugged him and then my aunt good-bye, gathered the CDs and a planter of pansies, and climbed into my car.

As soon as I had driven out of the parking lot, I began howling like a wounded animal. It was the kind of plaintive wail one hears on Discovery Channel specials capturing footage of baby elephants grieving for their freshly poached mothers.

It seemed natural to howl. After all, I had howled when I left my mother's womb forty-five years earlier to come into a strange new world; why wouldn't I howl now, as I was being thrust again into a new and terrifyingly unfamiliar world—but this time, without her?

Oh my God, I thought. *These are the first moments of my motherless life.*

"Mom," I cried out, "I'm so sorry. I'm so sorry you died. Please don't go. Please come back. Please stay. I'm not ready. I'm not."

And I wasn't ready. I had no idea how overwhelming grief could be—how I would ever feel at home in the world without her, and how much else I would have to grieve in addition to my mother in order to truly grow up. My mother's death called into question everything I thought I knew about myself—where I had come from, where I was going, and whom I belonged to. And all I knew for sure was that nothing and no one made sense now that the metaphorical umbilical cord that anchored me—for better and for worse—had been unarguably and unalterably severed.

DAVID

How could I not have noticed just how adorable he was? I must have been so focused on getting Alan to see my point during our couples' counseling sessions that I'd hardly had time to glance at the referee. But those sessions had ended. And now here I was—sitting alone on the couch directly across from him, absorbing the gaze from his soulful blue eyes, and wondering what I had been missing.

Despite having been a lifelong self-improvement junkie, I had felt an unprecedented urgency since my mother died to once and for all get life right—to live bolder, brighter, and better than ever before—though I had no idea what that might look like and felt less equipped than ever to find out. Mired in grief, I was convinced my problems would be solved if only I had my mother back and my husband the way I imagined a husband should be. Despite our best efforts, our three-year marriage hadn't quite found its footing. Not only were we a freshly blended family with kids and pets, but I had been the self-appointed healer-in-residence. Now my own wounds needed healing. In fact, I was in such despair that we agreed to put our couples' counseling on hold while I tended to my issues.

Since therapy had helped me through troubled times before, I hoped it would again. During our couples' therapy, David impressed me with his ability to connect with both Alan and me and his penchant for offering practical suggestions, not just psychobabble, when we got stuck. My decision to work with him individually was sealed after he shared that he too had lost a beloved parent to cancer. Perhaps he would understand more viscerally what I was going through.

His third-floor office, cocooned in a converted Victorian house—the house of my dreams—smelled cozy, like pinecones. My hands were sweating and my heart was pounding. He was just my type: dark hair, wire-rimmed glasses, a trim physique and boyish grin masking an impish and intelligent curiosity. He asked me about my relationship with my mom and if I was sharing my sorrow with Alan, while I was thinking about how nicely that tweed jacket fit him. He looked at me with what felt like an unprecedented intensity and listened to me with a rapt attention that threatened to unwrap the gooey, gory, and oh-so-tender places deep inside me.

So I began therapy with David, hoping for a psychic sanctuary. What I didn't expect was to immediately find myself thinking obsessively about him between sessions, planning the outfits I'd wear to my appointments, and wondering if he preferred chocolate chip cookies with or without nuts.

Yes, I did want to heal. But, I also wanted to curl up in his lap and purr.

PROMISES TO KEEP

When I was a child traveling with my family by car, my mom would read billboards and street signs out loud. I don't believe she knew she was doing it. Yet whether singing Gershwin while cooking brisket or sharing her opinion on topics ranging from troop levels in Afghanistan to the strength of the Phillies' bullpen, if Mom thought it or read it, she said it.

This was especially true of issues she felt strongly about.

A few summers before she died, while my mother and I were driving to my aunt's vacation home on Long Beach Island, Mom paused from narrating billboards long enough to mention a book she had recently read about end-of-life issues.

Even though I was driving and Mom was in good health, she pulled the book from her beach bag and asked me to read it when I had time. She said it echoed her philosophy of keeping gravely ill patients well informed of their condition so they could make meaningful treatment decisions. Mom believed that doctors and families were often biased toward extending life, even at the expense of a person's quality of life, and she was not interested in such compromises.

Since this wasn't the breezy summer conversation I had been expecting, I nodded politely and reached for the radio. But before I touched the power button, Mom grabbed my hand, turned to face me directly, and said, "Cheryl, if I am ever in that situation, I want you to promise me two things: first, that you will be honest with me no matter what."

"And"—still holding my hand—"that you will pluck the hairs on my chin if I can't do it myself."

Never more eager for her to resume narrating billboards, I quickly assured her that I would follow her wishes, never imagining that a little more than two years later I would be called to honor them.

My mother was a healthy, vibrant, nonsmoking sixty-seven years old when she was diagnosed with stage IV lung cancer. Only six and a half months later, she was dead.

It is still impossible to know whether it was the cancer, its treatment, or the side effects, that contributed to her swift, merciless decline. Because she fought so hard from the get-go, striving with all her might to make it two more years to celebrate her fiftieth wedding anniversary and her grandson's bar mitzvah, Mom didn't spend a lot of time dwelling on death.

The moment I learned about her cancer, I vowed to myself to accompany her on this rocky march into unknown territory in a way that allowed her to feel emotionally supported, physically cared for, and loved. And, of course, to keep the promises I had made just a few years earlier.

My desire to support Mom through her treatment went to uncanny lengths, as I often developed side effects similar to the ones she was experiencing. For instance, when she became constipated from the chemotherapy, I did too. When she developed a hacking cough, I developed one—though not as virulent as hers. At one point, two different doctors unknowingly prescribed each of us the same antibiotic for our symptoms. I suppose this physical acting out was my version of sympathy pain.

About two months into Mom's treatment, I noticed that one of the steroids she was taking increased the growth of her facial hair. I agonized about mentioning something as seemingly insignificant as propagating chin hairs; after all, by this time she was too weak to walk to the bathroom, so I doubted she had looked in the mirror in weeks, and the thought of giving her even a moment's worth of additional discomfort made me cringe. Yet I also knew Mom's only two vanities were maintaining her candy-apple-red fingernails and a fuzz-free chin.

So, because I had those promises to keep, I went to the nursing home the following Sunday afternoon when I knew no one else would be visiting. I fed her a Wendy's Chocolate Frosty—her favorite icy indulgence. Afterward, I massaged her hands and feet with the Crabtree & Evelyn rose-scented lotion a friend had brought and listened to her sensical and nonsensical musings with equal levels of interest.

Then I took a deep breath and asked, "Mom, do you remember asking me to pluck your chin hairs if there was ever a time you couldn't do it for yourself?"

"Yes," she replied. And before I could utter another word, she pleaded with me to pull them out.

So I reached into my purse for the tweezers I had packed that morning, just as she offered up her chin, reminding me of my fifteen-year-old cat when she presents her whiskered face, hoping for a scratch.

My hand trembled as I grabbed hold of the first hair, then counted out loud, "One . . . two . . . three," closed my eyes, and pulled. I felt as nervous as a novice heart surgeon. But compared with the battering and bruising Mom had already endured, this was as benign as brushing her teeth. In fact, she quickly began cheering me on, insisting that I wasn't hurting her and imploring me to get every last unwelcome hair.

My hesitancy turned to determination. And with Mom's confidence and my mighty Tweezerman, we worked as a team to remove every last hair. Just as important, we achieved a momentary yet satisfying victory over the indignity of cancer.

The next promise was more difficult to keep.

Three months later, my dad and I met with the oncologist to discuss my mother's condition. She had not responded well to her recent treatment, and we were concerned about both her steep decline and whether she was strong enough to endure a second round of chemotherapy.

The doctor, who at our first appointment had proclaimed, "I'm in it to win it," looked at Mom's recent test results and conceded that further treatment would not be possible. He estimated she had between two and four weeks to live.

Silently, my dad and I retreated to his car to absorb the unabsorbable. Dad began crying, and I began biting the inside of my cheek so as not to cry; one of the unilateral rules I had made for myself was that I wouldn't cry if he was crying.

A few minutes later, I said we should go tell Mom this news. Until now, my parents and I had consistently agreed on next steps, so I was unprepared when my father said, "No. We can't tell Mom. It's better if she doesn't know."

And I, thinking of what Mom had asked of me just two summers before, inhaled deeply and said, "We have to tell her. It's what she wants."

After a long, staggering silence, my dad put his head in his hands and said, "Cheryl, I couldn't live with myself if I told her."

But because of the promises I'd made, I whispered, "Dad, I couldn't live with myself if I didn't."

❀

Mom was always a first-rate planner. It was as predictable as it was comical that on our way home from visiting my brother in Georgia for Thanksgiving, several years before she got sick, she would start discussing where we would gather next year and who would begin scouting hotel and air fares. Still, nothing could have prepared me for what happened when my dad and I visited that afternoon, both still rattled from our earlier conversation.

We arrived to find my mom's older sister, Sandy, sitting at the end of the bed. Mom quickly greeted us and announced, "Good, we're all together. There are some things I want to discuss." And without the slightest hesitation, she began talking as if she had been in the doctor's office with us that very morning.

I prayed that my dad would not change the subject to something—anything—more tolerable. To his credit, he listened intently and began gently stroking Mom's arm.

She began raising previously taboo questions: How will I know I'm dying? What do I do when it's time to die? Will you be here with me at the moment of my death?

Next, she dictated a list of the lists she wanted made: Who will make meals for Dad when I am gone? Which caregivers should I write thank-you notes to? Whom can I ask to speak at my memorial service? Who should receive specific pieces of my jewelry? And what phone numbers will Dad need to help him take care of the house? Mom was the most lucid she had been in weeks, and the most lucid she would ever be again.

Dumbfounded and horrified that we were actually having this conversation, I forced myself to stay composed and address each of her questions and concerns with all the honesty and clarity that I could muster. Just as I had promised.

At one point, when I realized I was holding my breath, I reached for my aunt's hand and wiped away some of my long-denied tears. It was impossible to believe this was actually happening. *My mom* was fervently yet gently telling us she was ready to turn her fierce fight for life into a conscious surrender to death.

This was my mother's last conscious gift of caregiving. Mom knew, perhaps before we did—perhaps even before the doctor did—that she was dying. The signs were as clear to her as the billboards she read on our road trips. She also knew my dad and I would need each other in unprecedented ways after she died. So she stepped in and resolved the conflict that just hours before had threatened our previously trouble-free alliance.

Clearly, Mom too had promises to keep.

LOSING IT

Ten days into my motherless life, and I know already that I am not going through grief—grief is going through me. I am not in charge, which is quite disturbing, since I like being in charge. Not only that, but while my mother left lots of lists for what and whom she wanted taken care of after she died, the one list she didn't leave was the one telling me what to do with myself without her.

So I decide to purge, to get rid of as much stuff as I can as quickly as I can. After all, if someone so essential to my life can leave without permission, then it seems only fitting to try to reclaim some control by making my own decisions about what I can and cannot live without. And it is much easier to start with actual objects than with people, attitudes, or dreams.

I take a top-down approach and begin in my bedroom and bathroom: knee-highs, single earrings, sample-size hair conditioners, a tangle of unworn scarves, expired medicines, and hair clips—all go. In a large carton of handbags, I find a small summer satchel Mom gave me before she was sick. I never use it, because it doesn't have a zipper and I learned the hard way how untrustworthy zipperless bags are, but I've kept it because it's cute and it was from her. But seeing it now spawns an uncharacteristic act of aggression, and I hurl the purse across the room into the Goodwill pile. Take that! I don't want her zipperless purse. I want her.

Two minutes later, I am overcome by guilt and rush to retrieve the purse. I will give it to my nine-year-old niece, who will probably love it as much for the fact that it doesn't have a zipper as because it is from her granny.

Next I go into my home office. One year ago, Mom was helping me pick the paint color for this room. We chose Gleeful—the name alone made us both smile. Mom bought me two hand-painted water goblets and a picture frame to complement the candy-apple-green walls and celebrate my new space. She understood how much it meant for me to have a room of my own in our house and took as much delight as I did in decorating it. Because I've been in the office only one year, there isn't much to remove—just a few binders from presentations I made long ago, and cat toys more tempting to my dog, Gracie, than to my cats. Still it feels good to get rid of them.

As I move my dedicated whirl of activity into the kitchen, I sigh—momentarily wishing I were the kind of person whose grief response includes falling utterly and unapologetically apart. Last week, the oil company sent me a check saying I had paid them twice. Even my falling apart is just an amped-up version of holding it together.

I open the refrigerator, pour myself a glass of decaffeinated diet iced tea, and gulp three extra-strength Tylenol to quiet my pounding headache. It seems as if my body is in withdrawal. My muscles ache. Is it the flu? I feel queasy most of the time. This is 100 percent worse than when I quit smoking. At least then I was able to suck handfuls of fruit-flavored LifeSavers—but now my lifesaver is gone. And nothing quells my craving. I want to kick myself for all the times I was the first one to pull away from our hugs. I'd give anything to feel her arms around me now, to stroke her soft, silky hands. Clearly, this is not like summer camp, where I survived my homesickness by counting down the days until I could see her again, using a calendar she had taped to the inside cover of my trunk. Now I count the days since she left.

I am briefly buoyed when I discover three jars of Dijon mustard—each one hiding on a separate shelf in the pantry. I take out two of them, along with two cans of expired minestrone soup, evaporated milk, orange Jell-O, and a Cup Noodles that I must have brought from my single-girl kitchen. I pile all of the food that is still good but not necessary into a bag for our local food cupboard.

Maybe the reason I'm getting rid of all this stuff is to make more room for something to replace it—something other than sorrow—although there seems to be no space in my head to imagine anything new and tangible. There is only room for questions—simple questions that if she were here now I would ask, like: How much red wine did you put in your chicken cacciatore? Who did you share her first kiss with? What was I like as a four-year-old? And bigger questions, like: Where are you now? How can I live in a way that would make you proud? What's the purpose of my life if I am going to die? How can I get Dad through this? Who will take care of me when I'm too old to care for myself? What's the fucking point?

Enjoying a temporary sense of progress—masking what I fear will be a permanent sense of longing—I decide to tackle the nondescript cardboard boxes stashed in the coat closet. I open the closet door and gasp when I see Mom's black-and-purple tweed jacket splayed on the floor. It must have fallen off the hanger. It was the only piece of her clothing I took for myself. Mom loved wearing this jacket, and she looked radiant in it. It was custom-made for her by a textile artist Mom and Dad met at a craft show they enjoyed attending every year. I remember Mom's exuberance when she told me about the artist and described the fabric she chose for the coat. She was delighted when it arrived two months later. She even enjoyed showing off the little hidden pocket that was sewn into the inside lining.

When Dad and I were going through her closet, Dad urged me to take the coat, as it would make Mom happy. And I couldn't imagine giving it away. It was too "her." So I had it tailored and hung it in my closet, not knowing when I'd actually be ready to wear it myself—afraid that if I did, it would be another reminder that she wasn't coming back for it. But now, when I see the jacket lying in a heap on the floor, I hurriedly pick it up, put it on, and dive into a box of wrapping paper and bows.

Even though I am doing all the things people tell me to do when grieving—like walking, journaling, going to therapy, wearing fuzzy slippers, reading books on resilience—it still hurts like hell.

In fact, a fresh wave of grief blindsided me just yesterday. I had sent an email to a client where I asserted myself more strongly than I would have before Mom died. Two minutes later, the client emailed me a very positive response. And I felt proud. But only for a moment. The next thing I knew, I was weeping, realizing I couldn't call her to share my victory. I wanted to say, *Look, Mom. Look what I did. See what a big, brave girl I'm becoming?* But clearly I'm not big and brave enough yet to feel happiness or joy or pride or anything positive without its being usurped by wanting her.

At the end of the day, when I have purged, boxed, and bagged up all I can, Alan comes home from work and trips over a bag labeled GOODWILL.

"What have you been up to, and why are you wearing a coat?" he asks.

"It's Mom's jacket. I'm keeping it but getting rid of everything else I don't need anymore."

"Oh. Are you planning on keeping me?" he asks, half-jokingly.

I know I should laugh or hug him reassuringly, but instead I walk past him to take a bag of trash into the garage.

Which reminds me, I think I've lost my sense of humor.

EYE CONTACT

Something insidious invades every one of my sessions with David like a piece of spinach stuck in my teeth. We both know it's there, but I can't seem to get it out.

The intrusive issue is eye contact. Or, more specifically, my lack of eye contact. Well, even that's not specific enough. I have no trouble looking at David when he is speaking. In fact, I eagerly and vigilantly look directly into his eyes—desperate not only to hear what he is saying but also to intuit what he's thinking and feeling.

Sometimes when he speaks, I practice memorizing every feature of his face so that when I'm not in session and want to be with him, I can easily retrieve his image. Other times when I look at him, I imagine sending a warm beam of love directly from my heart into his heart.

Looking at David, and most anybody else who is speaking, comes easily and naturally. I developed my finely tuned antenna as a child. Reading other people's dispositions through their eyes (especially my father's) was a matter of survival.

But when it comes to looking David in the eye when *I* am sharing, I can hardly do it. I sporadically, fleetingly peek. Then my eyes dart away as if I've stumbled upon a neighbor's quarrel.

This problem does have its benefits, however. For instance, I can recall in great detail the pattern on the soles of David's shoes, which proved especially useful the day I informed him he had a piece of gum stuck on the bottom of his left loafer. And I know the country my coffee cup was made in and that the manufacturers want me to recycle the cup when I'm done. And I can recite the title of nearly every book on David's shelves and predict the exact spots on the couch where the sunlight will fall based on the time of our session.

But what I can't do with any regularity or comfort is look at him looking at me when I speak. It's a humiliating quirk that I can't hide the way I do my off-key singing voice or poor math skills.

Because it is often the proverbial elephant in the room, and because he is the kind of therapist who hunts down elephants with vigor and aplomb, we have discussed it a great deal. And I have offered a litany of reasons why I can't look at him—the most notable of which is the shame and unworthiness I fear he will see in my gaze. And then, of course, I feel ashamed of my shame, which only exacerbates my suffering. Since I couldn't offer David eye contact, I thought I'd offer him a list instead:

Dear David,

Why making eye contact with you is so perilous for me:
1. *Looking at me will hurt or kill you.*
2. *Looking at you looking at me will enhance my longing for you.*

3. *Looking at you looking at me will enhance my grief.*

4. *Not only am I afraid of what I'll see when I look at you, I'm just as afraid of what I won't see. If I see compassion, I'll want more of you; if I don't see compassion, I'll die inside—like I did as a child.*

5. *I'm afraid of what I'll feel.*

6. *I'm afraid you can't handle my feelings, especially fear, sorrow, anger—okay, all of 'em.*

7. *I'm afraid of feeling vulnerable.*

8. *I'm afraid of looking ugly.*

9. *I'm afraid you will leave me if you see me.*

10. *I'm afraid you will fire me.*

11. *I'm afraid it will feel bad.*

12. *I'm afraid it will feel good, and that will be worse.*

13. *I will dissolve.*

14. *I won't want to leave.*

15. *I will die of longing.*

To add insult to injury, I feel terrible that I can't do this one little thing for David. It must be awful for him. Eye contact is the only thing he has explicitly asked me to give him other than money, and I can't do it. And he tells me he wants me to look at him only for my sake, not his.

One day he suggested we practice eye contact (which felt beyond embarrassing) by having me choose a neutral subject to talk about. I tried discussing the plot of my favorite movie. *How hard could it be?* I thought. Even a kid can look another person in the eye when talking about a movie.

My favorite movie is *Witness*. Harrison Ford plays a Philly detective who recovers from his wounds, physical and otherwise, on an Amish farm where he is also protecting the key witness to a crime, an Amish boy. And in the midst of the crime drama, Ford's character falls in love with the boy's mother, and she with him.

In retrospect, I can't believe I thought this would be a benign topic. How could I not see the relevance of one of the key themes being unfulfilled longing, the use of eye contact to convey that longing, and the movie being called *Witness*, for G-d's sake? My unconscious was in overdrive. I felt unwrapped. I wanted to simultaneously run into his arms and out of his office.

Needless to say, while the movie did prove fertile in terms of my discussing these all-too-relevant themes with David, it was futile in facilitating my ability to sustain eye contact with him.

Another time we explicitly practiced eye contact, I chose what I thought was surely an innocuous topic. I started describing the big, grassy hill at the end of my street—the hill I walk Gracie down every day, the hill that reminds me of watching the opening scene of *The Sound of Music* as a child, and the hill where I recited a poem in honor of my mother every day the first year after she died.

It didn't take more than a few moments to realize that even this grassy hill meant something to me. Something I was afraid for him to see, which, I was coming to realize, was just about anything. And as quickly as I could say "doe, a deer," my eyes darted to the floorboards once again.

Everything is at stake when I look at him, no matter what I'm talking about. *Everything*. It seems there is nothing I can talk about that isn't charged for me, because I am the one doing the talking. It is me he has to see. And me who has to see him seeing me!

Which leads to this: eye contact is really about "I contact"—I making contact with David. Not only that, but eye contact is a metaphor for how I do life and how I do relationships. I can focus and attend to someone else, I can make that person feel safe and seen and special, but I can't receive that same kind of attention in return. I refuse to see my own eyes reflected in his.

❦

Now, here's the thing that makes this make complete and tragic sense. I didn't just pick this insidious disability out of a hat. I learned it from my father. I was his apprentice. My father cannot sustain eye contact either.

My dad could not, would not, does not look at me when he speaks to me. He will do only momentary glances, just like I do with David.

How does a little girl make sense of this? Unfortunately, it was painfully easy for me. She believes that the reason her daddy can't look at her (let alone hold her, play with her, console her) is that she is hideous to look at. It will hurt him. It could even kill him. And she concludes she must be quite ugly and/or very bad to be unworthy of her father's gaze.

Fast-forward forty years, and this same girl is now a woman, sitting across from her therapist, wanting him to love her into wholeness but convinced that her very glance will kill him, convinced that if he sees her—really sees her—one of them will die.

Last week I asked David if he truly knows how hard it is for me and what he's asking me to risk when he asks me to peek. Does he understand that a part of me desperately wants to be seen, and another part of me desperately wants to flee? And he replied, more softly than usual, "I know." I wanted to weep.

The few times I *have* actually sustained eye contact with David have felt moving beyond words—more intimate than sex. And in those moments I wonder if something can break my heart and heal it at the same time.

UNAVAILABLE: A BRIEF HISTORY

OF MY NOT-SO-ROMANTIC LIFE

This is the sordid history of my sometimes funny, often painful, rarely nourishing, pre-Alan romantic life. It includes a
smattering of crushes and Peter Pans, a litany of unavailable but
oh-so-compelling father figures, and a confession of the nifty but
self-defeating test I used to determine if a man was right for me.

CRUSHES

Billy: a teammate on my brother's Little League baseball team. I
think the only reason I had a crush on him was that he had one
on me and that felt good. I still have a copy of the handwritten
note he asked my brother to give me after a game. In it he asked
if (at the ripe old age of eight) I had ever kissed a boy. I had not.

Scott Baio: When I was twelve, I bet my best friend $100
that I would marry Scott Baio, from the TV show Happy Days,
before she would marry Willie Aames, of Eight Is Enough.

Kevin: the maintenance man/boy who worked at my summer camp. He looked like Donny Osmond. I volunteered to clear

the dirty dishes from my cabin's table at every meal just so I could watch him load the dishwasher.

Mr. Eleven: The private nickname my friend and I gave to the high school junior whose locker was next to mine. We called him that because it was his locker number and he was hotter than a ten.

Adam: By the time I arrived at college, I had perfected the art of the crush, so it was fitting that the name of my freshman dorm was Pinewood Hall. During my first two years of college, I pined most fervently for Adam, the shortstop on the baseball team. He wore his uniform one size too big and had marble-blue eyes, a welcoming smile, and a comfortable gait. He looked the way I wanted home to feel. I spent much of my free time perched at my dorm-room window, watching Adam cross the street that divided the residential from the academic parts of campus. My friends knew of my crush, and since it was a small school and one of my roommates was dating the team's first baseman, Adam knew too, which only added to my humiliation on the rare occasions we were actually in the same place at the same time.

PETER PANS

Eddie: A twenty-five-year-old graduate student eight years older than I was. With his prematurely receding hairline and close-set, bulging eyes, he looked like a lizard, which was all too appropriate, as he had a predatory tongue. I just wanted to cuddle and kiss, but Eddie quickly began campaigning for sex so we could "maintain our bond" when I was away at college. He made his argument most forcefully on an afternoon when we were lying on a faded leather couch in his parents' basement. What started out as playful wrestling turned much more threatening when he pinned me and said, "Finally. Right where I want you" while tug-ging at my jeans. I'm fairly certain that, had it not been for his brother's early return from school, I would have been raped. The next day, Eddie told me I wasn't ready for a "real relationship" and dumped me.

Peter: my first college boyfriend, and the man I gave my virginity to. Peter was a college administrator and twelve years my senior. Since it was against school policy for faculty or staff to be sexually involved with students, only my closest friends knew we were a couple. It felt good having the attention of an older man—one who owned his own condo and wore cologne and suits. I felt special knowing he was willing to break the rules to date me, yet also ashamed when he treated me like just another student when we were on campus. Peter said I was the easiest person in the world to be with and called me Doc, for the way I listened and helped explain him to himself. He also declared, only half-jokingly, that he would never be interested in a woman over thirty years old. Despite this, I fell despairingly in love with him. I couldn't let him go, even after I moved back to Pennsylvania to attend graduate school, even when longing for him was making me miserable, and even when my mother pleaded with me to stop taking his calls—calls asking me to be his friend while he began pursuing a fresh crop of coeds. I continued my pattern of dating broken men well into my late twenties and thirties.

Eric: At the end of our first date, Eric enveloped me in a bear hug and declared that I was "the one" for him. And since his first name contained the same four letters as my last name, and since my mother "just knew" she would marry my father the mo-ment she laid eyes on him, I believed lightning had struck twice.

It didn't matter that he was consumed by his work and lived a thousand miles away, and that most of our marathon phone calls involved my counseling him about his struggles with his jerk of a boss and roommates who just didn't respect his space. Four months later, an hour before my flight home from a passion-filled weekend visit, he confessed to dating a woman who lived in his neighborhood and said he wanted to break up. I answered yes through my tears when the airline attendant placed a pack of Kleenex on my lap and asked if someone had died.

FATHER FIGURES

The most blatant and regrettable type of unavailable men I dated were married. During my single years, I flirted with and had sexual contact with three, maybe four, married men. I say "maybe four" because one of them never admitted to being married but managed our courtship in such a way that I had deep suspicions he was. At the time, I worked in human resources and my job often necessitated private conversations with senior managers—most of whom were older, married men—about confidential employee issues. My empathetic and interested nature made it easy for me to build a rapport with these executives, and it didn't take long for some of the men to begin making more personal disclosures. One chief financial officer confided his desire to publish a crime novel he had been working on in secret for seven years. The day after I conveyed my enthusiastic support for his writing, he brought it in for me to read—all four hundred pages of it. Another executive began sharing his frustration with his wife's chronic disinterest in sex.

It was hard to resist the feelings of aliveness that came from my interactions with these men. They often commented on what a great listener I was and how gratifying it was to have me eagerly help them with their challenges—work-related or other. Being needed like that was so compelling—dare I say seductive—that I didn't notice that I was doing all the giving.

It was impossible not to develop a crush on some of these men—to wish I was the one they would go home to. And ultimately, with a few of them, I'm sorry to admit I was.

This is what I would say to the wives of these men if given the chance:

Dear wives of the three, maybe four, married men I had sexual contact with:

I am sorry.

I told myself that I wasn't cheating because I wasn't the one who was married. But while that's technically true, it doesn't let me off the hook. I cheated. I betrayed my own principles of right and wrong, I cheated you of time with your husband, and, most of all, I cheated myself of a real relationship.

I now know that women who feel good about themselves don't borrow other people's husbands.

I let my loneliness supersede my values and broke a code of sisterhood that I otherwise cherish. I wrongly believed that longing equaled loving, that clandestine was sexy, and that I must have been special if a man would break his marriage vow to be with me. But please know I was never special enough for him to leave you—or even to offer faint promises of leaving. (And even if he had, I most likely would have run for the hills!)

So while I can't change my past transgressions, I can offer my heartfelt apology for participating in them.

Sincerely,
Cheryl

FANTASY MAN

In addition to my childhood crushes, I invested in a very private and robust romantic fantasy life—one that initially provided an outlet for the forbidden and a substitute for the affection and attention that was unavailable to me growing up, yet eventually became a barrier to the real-life intimacy I both craved and feared.

While the face of Fantasy Man changed over the years, the fantasy itself stayed more or less the same: I would be going through my day in a voiceless, invisible fashion, when something would happen to put me at risk. Fantasy Man would see my peril, jump into action, save me from harm, and then pull me into a sheltering embrace.

In my early thirties, I even started a journal to Fantasy Man. I kept it under the theory that if I wrote to him, he would come. And when he did show up, I was sure he'd want to know all about who I was and what I was up to during those years. Most of the entries were bland accountings of my day, but some of them included musings about what he might be doing at that very moment and how much sweeter our life together would be since we had waited so long to find each other.

Relegating my love life to my imagination had two primary benefits: first, it allowed me to stay loyal to my father, the man in my life most in need of healing due to the effects of a devastating childhood, and second, it kept me safe from the risks of a real relationship.

It was also quite ironic that while I doggedly held on to my fantasy of a welcoming and sheltering hero who would see my vulnerability and comfort me, in reality I did all I could to mask my vulnerability and push away men who had the capacity to actually see and give to me, and instead tried to fill the role of savior for them.

THE TEST

During my dating years, I developed a test to determine if I would go out with a man a second time. I called it the Me/Why Me Test. It went like this: After we settled into our seats, I would quickly take control of the conversation and start asking my date questions about himself. Part one of my test was to see how long the subtle interrogation continued before my date noticed that he had been doing all of the sharing. He earned one point for noticing, and a second point for noticing within the first five minutes. He could earn a third point by asking *me* a question, and a fourth point if he asked a follow-up question, rather than turning the conversation back to himself.

The test allowed me to learn a lot about my date and make him feel good about himself while revealing little about myself. Inevitably, the next day I'd call a friend to complain about my date's self-centeredness—not revealing how I had manipulated the entire interaction.

If you don't believe you are worthy of receiving attention and you are terrified of anything even approximating intimacy, this is the test for you. It works every time.

ROCK BOTTOM

Up until this point in my dating history, I had always been with men, available or not, who were likable and in their own ways kind. But what finally ended my string of poorly chosen romantic partners was a series of interactions—the word "affair" would be too generous—with a married coworker who was so miserable, critical, and eventually abusive that he is not even worthy of a pseudonym.

The weekend after a particularly degrading encounter with him, I cried for two days straight. Finally, I called a close friend and confessed every horrid detail. I declared that I would rather be alone forever than continue subjecting myself to this kind of suffering. I had hit bottom, and I was ready to accept that I had gotten there because that's where I had put myself. That's where I thought I belonged—on the bottom, on the outside, in the shadows. I also realized that while I had been with a lot of men, not a lot of men had been with me—meaning, I had kept myself as unavailable to them as they were to me. Again, I was acting from a place of deep unworthiness and shame, convinced I was destined to be the favorite aunt and friend, always the bridesmaid and a true standout in the Land of Misfit Toys. But this last indignity called forth the faint hope of something more—something better—or at least something else. I had had enough. I vowed to do whatever it took to change my ways.

THE TRANSITIONAL GOOD GUY

This subheading and the aforementioned vow might lead you to believe that my not-so-romantic life took a 360-degree turn toward bliss. You would be wrong. Read on.

I met Daniel, one of the best good guys at a speed-dating event, where fifteen women sit at individual cocktail tables and fifteen men sit across from them. The event organizers ring a bell, and each pairing has four minutes to talk and decide if they have any interest in each other. At the end of the four minutes, the bell rings, each person marks yes or no on his or her private score sheet, and the men rotate tables. This goes on until each woman and man have spent four minutes talking with each other. At the end of the evening, you hand in your scorecards, and the next day the event organizers email you any yes-yes matches. Daniel was the last man I talked with and the only man I checked yes to, as he didn't let me get away with my one-sided inquisition and insisted on using most of our four minutes to learn about me.

Daniel brought me flowers on our first date. He genuinely liked my cats. He folded my laundry and went to see romantic comedies with me without complaining. He enjoyed spending time with my parents, loved my body, meditated twice a day, and encouraged me to eat what I wanted. He was the guy my friends said I deserved. And for a while, I agreed—until I started picking fights with him just to create some familiar sparks of drama between us.

I was wholly unprepared for Daniel and was furious at him for liking me so much just for being me. My wiring said I should have to work for and earn love and attention. He wasn't asking me to fix or heal him, which was totally bewildering. In fact, I couldn't stand it. Love should feel perilous, passionate, unsafe, and exciting. It should be mixed with periods of longing and leaving and great makeup sex. He should be crying on my shoulder, asking me to explain himself to him. Love shouldn't be this comfortable. Not even for a moment.

Despite Daniel's talking about what our collective future might look like, I knew we wouldn't get there when I started asking friends if he was really as good-looking as my mother said he was and began looking for excuses to stay home alone with my cats, heat up some turkey meatballs, and watch *Entertainment Tonight*.

GRIEF GAMES

1. Mom, if you can hear me, let there be three plane trails in the sky.

2. Mom, if you can hear me, send the little blue bird that is on the tree limb outside my office down to my window.

3. Mom, if you are listening, please visit me in my dream tonight.

4. Here's how I'll beat this grief: I'll have a baby of my own, and then I won't miss you this much.

5. If I have an affair with David, I won't miss you this much.

6. If I have a baby with David, I definitely won't miss you this much.

7. If I go back to the nursing home where you last lived, I will find you playing bridge with the other residents.

8. I bought a new, down-filled, hypoallergenic pillow so I can replace my bad dreams with good ones about being with you.

9. I start each morning with a whiff of the half-filled bottle of Jo Malone Amber & Lavender cologne you wore. This magically brings you back to me . . . for a moment.

10. I call your house just so I can hear your voice on the answering machine. (Each time, I'm afraid of disturbing Dad. My entire life—afraid of disturbing Dad.)

11. It is my birthday—the first birthday of my life without a card from you. I can't bear it. I go into the basement and dig out three old birthday cards from you and weep.

12. I imagine a repository where motherless adult daughters can sign up to be adopted by a nurturing, mom-like woman. Like the way our local paper spotlights a young child in need of a loving family every Tuesday.

13. I remember that Dad is out of the house, teaching. I call your house and record your outgoing answering-machine message onto my iPhone. Now I can listen

to your voice as much as I want without bothering
Dad. It lasts all of eleven precious seconds: "Hi, this
is the Rices', and we're very glad you called. Please
leave us a message after the beep. Thanks very much.
Bye-bye."

14. This is how I mark time. It is July 1, three months
since you died. It is July 15, three months and two
weeks since you died. It is February 1 . . .

15. If I stop eating and get really sick, you will come
back to feed me.

LOVE AND LONGING

As my free fall into grief deepened, my infatuation with David, my therapist, flourished. Three months into our work, I walked into his office, sank into his love seat, and blurted in a soft, staccato voice, "I think I am in love with you."

Without missing a beat, he replied, "Wow. That's a big-deal feeling and an even bigger deal to say to anyone, let alone your therapist."

I could feel my face redden. I wanted to run away, but before I could move, David continued. "Cheryl, look at me." My eyes had fixated on the lid of my coffee cup. "I think you are very brave, self-aware, and smart. You are a beautiful person with many attractive qualities."

I knew his next sentence would not be good. I knew it would include a "but."

"That said, I don't have affairs. And even if someday I get divorced and you get divorced, we still would not be together. In fact, there are no conditions that will ever allow us to have anything other than a doctor-patient relationship. But I will always be here for you as your therapist."

The tears that had been welling up spilled down my cheeks. I reached for a tissue to dab lightly at my eyes—not wanting to ruin my makeup or add to my humiliation by openly sobbing or blowing my nose.

Before the interminable session was over, David reminded me about transference—the tendency for patients to project childhood feelings for parents onto their therapist. He said mine was "thick," meaning the depth of my feelings for him represented the depth of other unfulfilled longings in my life—especially those from my childhood. David proposed I commit to our work for at least another ten weeks. Not the proposal I had wanted, but a proposal nonetheless. And I accepted.

KELLY

I was bobbing in a stew of grief and longing. My homesickness for my mom was unrelenting. My crush on David was mounting. My dream of a perfect marriage was dissolving. And in my continued (and often misguided) attempts to find comfort, I found myself reaching back into the past. Her name was Kelly.

It had been fourteen years since our last communication, and I knew from previous attempts to contact her that it was unlikely she would respond. Still, I thought it was worth a try. Despite having wonderful friends in my life now, I longed to hear her voice, tell her about my mom's passing, and receive her special kind of kindred comfort that I still remembered so well. Kelly adored my mom. She loved to talk to her about books and boys during the countless hours she spent at my house. She often bemoaned the fact that, unlike my mom, hers was physically and emotionally distant. Maybe, just maybe, learning about my loss would compel her to put the past behind us, to come console me and be my friend again. Or maybe I was just reaching for a ghost.

I took out a piece of notebook paper.

Dear Kelly,

I know it's been a very long time since we last spoke, but there's something I want you to know. I'm sure you remember my mom. She adored you. And she died recently and nothing has been right since. In fact, her death cut me to pieces and I was hoping you could help put me back together again.

Kelly had been my best friend for over twelve years. We met the first day of class in graduate school. If there is such a thing as love at first sight in a platonic relationship, then that's what I felt for her.

We started talking when she sat next to me in Counseling Psychology, and we continued our conversation over lunch at a campus pub when class ended. I'm sure, in all the years I knew Kelly, we shared hundreds of meals, but it was that first lunch that is etched most indelibly in my mind: A booth by the window. Two cheeseburgers—mine with American cheese and hers with cheddar. We even felt comfortable enough with each other to split one order of fries. We talked easily about college friends, our childhoods, and our goals for life after graduate school. Our lunch lasted three hours. It felt like three minutes. It felt like home.

I had friends in college. Good friends. Friends I loved and who loved me. I would never have known anything was missing from these relationships or wanted for more (though, looking back, I know it is telling that I chose to do my senior thesis on learned helplessness and loneliness). But when I met Kelly, for the first time in my life I felt "gotten." I had always been the one who "got" other people—made them feel seen and understood while revealing little of myself. Now, Kelly was the "me" that I was for others. We quickly became that for each other, and the chronic low-grade loneliness that I had felt all of my life was at least partially allayed.

We were born weeks apart. We had younger brothers close in age. We had fathers we adored and longed for, though Kelly's father died when she was just six. Both of us grew up feeling like we belonged in the Land of Misfit Toys—too sensitive for our own good and dripping in unworthiness. I coped by being kind. She coped by being funny—she loved making self-deprecating jokes and singing silly songs.

One time, we went on a volunteer trip to repair trails in the Grand Canyon. It rained every day of the trip, but we entertained ourselves by crushing on the same trail leader. We imagined marrying and having children at the same time and even dreamed of sharing a shiny red Mazda Miata. We would each drive it every other month. We celebrated weekends and birthdays by going out dancing. We nurtured each other through breakups and were each other's first call after every date. In fact, Kelly was my greatest source of stability and comfort during the ups and mostly downs of my not-so-romantic life, and had no problem dropping whatever she was doing to share a meal of turkey meatballs and coffee ice cream when disaster struck.

After graduate school, we rented a two-bedroom apartment and lived together for two years, before Kelly got a better-paying job and moved into an apartment of her own closer to her work. During the next ten years, she moved three or four times, each time with help from her brother and me, as she couldn't afford to hire a moving company.

I began again:

Dear Kelly,

I'm sorry for starting a letter like this, but I don't know another way. My mom died, and I'm lost beyond words. I thought you might understand, or care, or want to be here for me as I would want to be there for you, despite all that has happened between us.

Ten years after we met, I applied to a competitive graduate program in organization development on the West Coast, and to my surprise was accepted. Though the program was based in California, it was designed for working professionals, so I had to be on campus for only eight weeklong classes over two years and didn't have to move.

The classes started in September, but, unbeknownst to me, a mandatory orientation was scheduled for a weekend in August—the same weekend Kelly and I had planned to go on a whale-watching trip to Cape Cod with a singles group. I felt terrible having to cancel and told Kelly that if she couldn't find another friend to take my place, I would pay the difference so she could have a single room and not have to bunk with a stranger, or I would reimburse her entirely if she decided not to go at all. It wasn't ideal, but it was the best I could do.

I knew Kelly would be disappointed (as was I), but I thought she would understand. We had always been supportive of each other's goals and considered ourselves lifelong learners. When I first told her about it, she was bummed but understanding and even started making a list of friends she could ask to take my spot. But the next day she called and, in a wholly unrecogniz-able, steely tone, told me she was deeply hurt by my decision to attend the orientation and would no longer be my friend. She asked me not to contact her ever again and hung up.

I felt as if I had been shot in the stomach with a cannon ball. I began to shake. *Oh my God*, I thought. *What have I done?* And, more important, how could I undo it?

Frantic, I called her back and left a message:

"Hey, Kel . . . I'm *so* sorry. I had no idea the orientation would get in the way of our trip. I had no idea I'd even get into the damn program! But I want to make things right. So please call me back as soon as you get this. We'll figure it out. I love you."

My next impulse was to drive to her home, but, in an uncanny twist of fate, Kelly had moved into a new apartment that same weekend. And to make matters worse, for the first time in her life, she had hired professional movers. So while I knew the town she had moved to, I didn't yet have her new address.

I left messages and notes for her at work apologizing for anything and everything I could think of, including canceling the trip and forgetting to return a pair of earrings she had loaned me. (The idea of being angry at her didn't even cross my mind. It would take years for me to even contemplate the possibility.) Kelly was mad at me, and it must be my fault. I had been a horrible friend, and I had been fired. All I wanted to do was rewind that day, rewind that conversation. Rewind the outcome and have my best friend back. It was the same urge I felt the day I learned I had to stay at camp for eight weeks, and the day the oncologist told my dad and me that Mom had just a few weeks to live.

I was still not happy with my letter. Maybe the third time would be the charm:

Dear Kelly,

I hope this note finds you well. Something really sad has happened, and it has me thinking about you and about our friendship. Or what I thought was our friendship. My mom died, and I can't believe how alone I feel. She adored you. You were the only one who ever came close to mimicking her accent just right. She used to laugh until she cried when you did. Do you remember that? Or have you buried those memories like I buried her?

Being dumped by Kelly was one thousand times worse than being dumped by any boyfriend. On some level, I always expected boys to break my heart, and I always expected my best girlfriend to help me mend it. Wasn't one of the unstated perks of having a best friend never having to be on guard for such a calamity? I thought I knew Kelly as deeply as I knew myself. I thought we were cut from the same cloth—frayed in the same ways but also bound tightly together by our wounds, our love for each other, and an unbreakable loyalty. I was certain our friendship was immune to such a betrayal.

I hoped after a few weeks Kelly would come to her senses and call me. I pictured us embracing in tears, falling to the floor laughing, and then, over a large spinach pizza and a bottle of zinfandel, carrying on our conversation as if nothing had happened. But the call never came.

I read the note over again. It was still not right.

Dear Kelly,

I'm wondering if the statute of limitations on being mad at me has expired. I really hope it has, as I could really use a hug from you. My mom died. And the weird thing is, I am missing you almost as much as I miss her. But last I checked, you're not dead and I feel this coursing urgency to talk to you again—to make things right. It still feels so very wrong. And, to make matters worse, I have fallen in love with my therapist (I can hear you laughing now!) and I wish you were here so you could help me laugh about it too. You always knew how to help me lighten up. Gosh, I could use some lightening up now, Kelly.

During the first year after Kelly fired me, I must have spent one hundred hours talking and crying about it with my mom. And while she had tremendous empathy for me, she also had no problem venting the anger toward Kelly that I was still incapable of. She begged me to see that it wasn't my fault and seemed visibly hurt when I blamed myself.

Mom also provided one of the only theories ever offered that even came close to making sense of Kelly's actions: Kelly had a deep fear of abandonment, due in large part to her father's death when she was a girl. She initiated the end of every relationship with a boyfriend before it got too serious or before the guy had a chance to leave her. I used to joke with her about how long I should set the timer on her latest suitor before the buzzer rang and she gave him the heave-ho. Never in a million years did I imagine my time too would one day expire. Surely I—her very best friend in the world—was exempt from expiration dates. But

Mom felt sure that Kelly was triggered not by the orientation I had to attend, but by her fear that my going back to school meant I was moving on without her. And instead of risking being left behind, she left me instead.

While my mother's theory made sense intellectually, it made absolutely no sense in my heart. I was *me*, for goodness' sake. Didn't Kelly know I would *never* leave her? And if she didn't know that, why couldn't she talk to me about her fears instead of acting on them so brutally?

After all these years, I still struggle not to blame myself. If only I hadn't gotten into the program. If only I had refused the orientation outright. If only she hadn't moved that very same weekend and I had gone to her apartment and camped out until we worked it out. It was reminiscent of the way I blamed myself for being banished to camp: if only I were good enough, kind enough, I wouldn't have been sent away.

The hurt from Kelly's dismissal was so acute, I don't think I've ever let myself melt into a friendship the same way. And I know it is one cause of the "one wrong move and I'm fired" fears that creep into my experience with David and my new family.

I think I have it!

Dear Kelly,

I know this is a lousy way to start a letter, but my mom died and she had this theory that I want to ask you about. She said the reason you ended our relationship so dramatically, and suddenly, and dare I say cruelly, was because you thought I was leaving you for graduate school and, because of your childhood abandonment, decided to leave me first. It would really mean a lot to me and the memory of my mom if you would tell me if she was right. You don't have to like me again—just please answer me.

I have never really given up hope that one day Kelly will miss me as much as I miss her and get in touch. But so far that day hasn't come.

I tried finding her on LinkedIn. Nothing. Facebook, nothing. I broke down and paid $36 to an online intelligence database to learn that she was living in Ohio and had worked in a hospice (which seemed quite fitting, if not ironic). I also found out that she had married. It wasn't clear if she had any children.

I even found an address.

Why is this so darn hard?

Hi Kelly,

Remember me, your best friend from Penn? We were going to raise our families next door to each other and share a sports car? Are you still mad at me? Have you thought about me? What do you think about when you think about me? Do you remember the Grand Canyon? Our dancing?

Is your best friend still your best friend if she deserts you—if she murders your friendship and never once looks back? Is the Kelly I wanted to write to the Kelly who was my best friend or the Kelly who killed our friendship? I can't imagine she could be both. How could I not have known?

I reread this letter and ripped it, along with all of the other attempts, into a ball and dumped it in the trash. I got it. Even though she was alive, Kelly was indeed gone. As gone to me as my mother—maybe more so. No letter was going to change that. Once again, my attempts to find sanctuary turned into another loss to be endured. There had to be a better way.

A DAUGHTER'S CHOICE

First: I am standing in the upstairs hallway of my childhood home. My mother is standing next to me. She is young, in her late thirties or early forties. She turns to me with a big, beautiful smile on her face and begins walking down the steps to the first floor of the house I grew up in.

Next: I am in the front yard. Gracie is with me. Suddenly I see a very large man with white hair. He is walking as if he has braces on his legs—a stiff monster walk. He is bad. He is coming to kill us.

I am in our house, but Gracie and Mom are still outside. I am screaming for both of them to run inside the front door. Gracie is in the front yard. Mom is on the right side of the house and doesn't see Monster Man, or if she does, she doesn't seem scared of him. I frantically scream for her and Gracie to come: "Mom! Gracie! Come. Come quick. Gracie, come! Hurry, please hurry, Mom!"

Monster Man continues approaching, his arms reaching straight out in front of him, preparing to snatch someone or something. Gracie finally heeds my call and dashes inside the house. Once she is safe, I slam the front door shut. Mom now sees Monster Man coming toward her. She is not listening to my pleas for her to run inside. And still she does not look scared or panicked. She looks beautiful. I am torn. Do I stay with Gracie or run outside to try to rescue Mom—and risk getting snatched myself?

Through a window in our house, I see our next-door neighbors, the O'Connors, and frantically beg them to help Mom. They see me but don't respond.

I am terrified. Monster Man is coming for Mom, and he will get her. I have failed to save her.

I wake up drenched in sweat and sorrow. When I recover and regain my bearings, it occurs to me that I saved Gracie and me and let Mom go. I chose life. And from the look on her face, Mom was ready to go; she was not afraid. Not only that, she didn't call out for me to save her but instead looked peaceful and relieved knowing I was safe, with Gracie in my arms.

Maybe I didn't fail her after all.

CALLING IN THE ONE

I was thirty-nine years old, tired of turkey meatballs, solo Sunday matinees, and making the same mistakes over and over again. I wanted to move forward, not just practically but also emotionally and spiritually, for I truly believed I had learned and experienced all I could as a single woman. It was time to dive into a new and deeper relational adventure. This meant divorcing the self-sabotaging behaviors I had been married to my whole life and opening up to real love—not fantasy love. (As it turned out, it was more a trial separation than a divorce.)

I started therapy to get my mental and emotional house in order, consulted a feng shui expert to get my physical house in order, spoke with a psychic, bought books on manifesting true love, said yes to invitations even when I didn't feel like it, and joined a smattering of singles groups.

After a few months, with nothing much to show for my efforts, I decided to cast a wider net and do something wholly original, wildly assertive, and potentially humiliating to call forth my man. I discussed a few options with my therapist at the time,

Caroline, who advised me to keep whatever I did light—even playful—so as not to reek of desperation.

So, with lighthearted yet purposeful intention, I penned the following email:

There once was a woman named Rice
Who was ready to roll marriage dice.
She was tired of solo,
And dating Mr. Oh No!
So she asked her dear friends for advice.

I have a special favor to ask you.

I would like to find someone wonderful to spend my life with. I'm doing my part by plunging into the world of online dating, singles mixers, and speed dating. However, I can't help but believe in the power of good old-fashioned matchmaking. So I'm writing to ask for introductions to quality single men.

And, just to keep things interesting, I will gladly make a charitable donation of $1,000 in the name of the person who introduces me to Mr. Right.

At 9:30 PM on March 18, 2004, my finger quivering at the keyboard, I pushed SEND and emailed my note to more than two hundred friends and acquaintances.

The following morning, Michael, a friend who lived in Arizona but, unbeknownst to me, happened to be doing business in Philly for the week, logged on to his computer and read my note.

A few hours later, as Michael was walking to a meeting, he bumped into Alan, whom he had not seen in more than ten years. As they caught up, Alan mentioned his pending divorce and desire to begin dating again. Without disclosing my email, Michael casually offered that he knew someone he thought Alan might like and gave him my name and phone number.

That afternoon, Alan called and asked me to dinner that evening. Even though I was delighted my email had garnered a reply so quickly, I had barely survived one too many bad blind dinner dates and suggested meeting at a local coffee shop instead.

At 7:00 PM on March 19, 2004, less than twenty-four hours after I sent my cyber-request for my soul mate, I met Alan. And the adventure began.

I was immediately taken by his rugged good looks: salt-and-pepper hair, warm brown eyes, wire-rimmed glasses, trim and strong body. He also had a firm handshake and the kind of big, boyish grin I was a sucker for. But moments into our conversation, the compelling combination of emotional strength and vulnerability that came pouring out of him eclipsed his physical presence.

Though Alan was deeply sad and even a bit ashamed his marriage had failed, he wasn't looking for pity and didn't drone on about his ex, as many previous dates had. Instead he focused on his passion for his young son and daughter, understandably his number-one priority. I was so moved when he shared that he had told his children it was he who had failed their mother, but that he would do everything in his power not to fail them, that I didn't even think to give him my "test."

I left that evening feeling a lot of compassion for Alan. He was indeed a good man with a big heart, but I also felt he was nowhere near ready for the serious relationship I was searching for. So I decided that the next day I'd start working through my list of eight other potential suitors. That email was very effective.

However, I didn't get further than a call to the next man on the list when Alan phoned to tell me that while I was the "whole package," he wasn't ready for the whole package. I told him I understood completely and wished him well.

Two hours later, Alan called me from his son's hockey game to ask me out to dinner the next night. Touched by his comical enthusiasm, I put aside my concerns about his readiness and accepted his invitation.

At the end of that date, I kissed him good night on the cheek and said that while he was a lovely person, it was clear he was just getting back on the dating highway, while I was in the fast lane—eager to find a husband and have a family of my own. It didn't seem right to ask him to speed up, and I wasn't ready to slow down. Maybe we should just be friends.

Sixteen months later, Alan proposed.

NURTURING NIRVANA

Despite my intentions to commit only to available men capable of true intimacy, I now faced an irresistible lure. Alan was the most charmingly handsome fixer-upper who ever came to my doorstep. Though he was by nature an optimist, his outer and inner life were in turmoil when we met. Practically, he needed to find a new home for himself and the kids, determine which physical and emotional belongings from his seventeen-year marriage to pack and which to leave behind, work out custody and divorce agreements with a disgruntled ex, and adjust to life as a single parent.

My well-honed helping and healing skills took to him like a duck to water. I jumped into planning-and-organizing mode, helping him pack, shop for new furniture, and navigate his move. And on days when he was feeling beaten up by thorny divorce proceedings or bitter voice mails from his soon-to-be-ex-wife, I soothed his wounded ego with a romantic dinner and a serving of passionate sex for dessert.

Since by this time I had a lot of experience nurturing damaged men, this was the Super Bowl of being needed—and not just by Alan, but also by his two young children and even his ex-wife, who would sometimes call me for support if she couldn't get through to Alan. I was in "helping heaven." I felt so powerful, potent, and alive that even doing his family's laundry felt sexy.

It didn't register at the time that Alan's primary interest in me seemed to be that I was primarily and wholly interested in him. In fact, when Alan and I met with the rabbi prior to our wedding, he asked us what we found attractive about each other. After I gushed about all I loved about Alan and his kids, the rabbi turned and asked Alan what he loved about me. Alan stuttered and stumbled and asked the rabbi to repeat the question—three times! He finally answered with a short list of things I had done for him and his kids—nothing about who or what he saw or valued in me, independent of him.

More concerned with Alan's stumbling pause than with his actual answer (after all, it felt so good to be needed that his inability to wax on about my good qualities was secondary), I emailed the rabbi later that day to ask if he had noticed Alan's delayed response as well. He said some men have a hard time talking about their feelings and that I should take it as one piece of a broader picture.

But by then the broader picture was that I was in love—with Alan, with his children, and with the feeling of being needed, and being needed equaled being worthy. So intoxicating were these feelings that I gleefully lost myself in wedding planning, home buying, and new-family building without considering what (and who) might be missing.

HUNGER

I t started out innocuously. When Mom was enduring chemo and radiation, I was too busy tending to her, my dad, and my own family to eat properly. As her health and appetite declined, I too, perhaps in an unconscious act of solidarity, became less interested in food. My appetite disappeared entirely immediately after she died. Over time, it slowly returned, but my ability and desire to feed myself did not. Before long, I was immersed in a silent war with hunger—a battle I knew from experience was a most worthy opponent.

Like many women, I had hated my body for as long as I could remember. Like a merciless bully, I pummeled it with re-lentless criticism; demeaning my shape, flesh, weight, height, breasts, legs, stomach, ass. It seemed only my wrists made it through unscathed.

My wrath began in earnest when I was a teenager. I was chubby—chubby enough to be called Thunder Thighs and Bowling Pin by the boy who lived in the house behind me. And though this taunting made me miserable, being overweight also served me well, as it kept me from having to deal with the positive attention of boys, which I learned early on was something to avoid.

One night a first-grade classmate, Timmy Grant, called our home, asking to speak to me. He probably wanted to continue the conversation we'd had that day about the merits of blue and green Play-Doh. My father, unprepared for the call, told Timmy I wasn't available and abruptly hung up. He then began teasing me, relentlessly repeating in a singsong first-grader voice, "Timmy likes Cheryl," over and over again. I felt deep shame, as if I had done something wrong, something bad to garner Timmy's attention and my father's teasing. Even though my dad was joking, and even though I was all of seven years old, I knew he did not approve. And in that moment, something seared into my brain—something it would take decades to challenge and sort out: I would lose my dad if I accepted the attention of a boy or, worse, admitted my own desires for one.

So while being overweight kept me safe and loyal to my father, it also cost me his acceptance. He was put off by fat people, fat women in particular. And he made it clear he did not approve of my weight in small but crushing ways, like refusing me dessert yet serving it to my brother, and by making comments like "I think you should wait for dinner to eat" or "Didn't you have french fries last week?" if he caught me opening the refrigerator or eating fried food.

My body loathing increased exponentially after puberty, when out of nowhere I started breaking out in hives from head to toe and everywhere—and I do mean *everywhere*—in between. For the uninitiated, these weren't just small, rash-like dots that could be covered with calamine lotion, but large, raised and raging patches of flesh that morphed my body into an itchy topographic map. Even my tongue, lips, eyelids, fingers, and toes ballooned. Scratching only made them multiply. I had to carry an EpiPen in my school backpack in case my throat closed.

After extensive testing, doctors diagnosed the hives as idiopathic, which meant there was no known cause for them and therefore no way to prevent them. The steroids that were prescribed to calm my raging skin brought on additional weight gain and mood swings. I felt like a freak. The outbreaks continued intermittently well into my young adulthood.

I wonder now if the hives weren't my body's way of giving voice to all the feelings I couldn't otherwise express—like anger and loneliness. And I also wonder if they weren't a desperate attempt for me to connect with my father, whose own body was taken hostage by chronic basal cell skin cancers.

In college I flirted more with diets than with boys, trying a buffet of laxatives, diet pills, and periodic purging. A college administrator, who probably thought he was helping me, told me once how beautiful my face was but said if I wanted a boyfriend I should lose weight.

Looking back, I'm surprised my body still serves me at all—that it actually moves and functions so ably—considering what I put it through.

After college, it seemed I flipped a switch because the extra weight came off quickly and relatively easily. Close friends didn't recognize me when I attended my one-year college reunion, and even I had to do double takes when passing a mirror.

But the funny/horrible thing is, I lost the weight but not the image. I shrank from a size 10/12 to a 2/4 but still felt fat. Even when I was training for a half marathon, regularly running five to ten hilly miles a day and garnering compliments on my toned legs or ample breasts from men I was dating, I didn't believe them. I often wondered, if a person is a size 2 but feels like a size 12, is it even worth losing the weight?

I spent years convinced that if my hips were just one or two inches closer, my entire life would come together. Ironically, Alan often tells me how much he loves my hips. He says they have magical properties in them. Go figure.

But despite my sordid history with my body, not eating after my mom died felt different. It wasn't about fitting into a new pair of jeans; it was about fitting into my life as a motherless daughter.

Enduring my hunger became a daily battle. Just as I had endured and battled homesickness all those years ago at camp, I now used those same skills to withstand my hunger pains. Each day began with a countdown until the arbitrary hour I allowed myself to eat, recording every morsel in a food journal and vowing after each day's entry to do better, i.e., eat less or exercise more the next day. My daily victory was falling into bed with my stomach churning— so loudly I worried it would wake Alan. (Like most husbands, Alan was more attuned to gained pounds than lost ones.)

For a while, the hunger pains felt good and I took pride in tolerating them. They were certainly, along with my fantasies of David, a welcome distraction and physical punctuation point for my grief. Moreover, the battle felt winnable, as opposed to the rest of my life, where I felt overmatched and overwhelmed— having no idea how to be happily married, heal my despondent father, or find the energy to build my coaching practice. And since there was no possibility of getting Mom's advice on fixing any of it, I chose to focus instead on something I could accomplish. Moving the number on the scale gave me a renewed sense of purpose.

Eventually, my best friend, Jane, shared her concerns about my weight loss. We were taking a walk one Saturday morning, when from out of nowhere she said, "Honey, you look really thin. You're losing your curves. I'm worried about you."

"I'm fine. What are you doing this weekend?" I replied, eager to change the subject. But Jane persisted. She knew too much about my history with food and weight. "I'm onto you. You're doing your disordered-eating thing. It's not good. Not now. You need nourishment." I wanted to tell her that my eating was as disordered as my life right now and that what she saw as problematic, I actually saw as a brilliant strategy—one that didn't hurt anyone else or cost money. It wasn't illicit or illegal. Quite the contrary—thinness is acceptable, even admirable. Plus, it's incredibly empowering to liberate oneself from food. But instead of making arguments I knew she would dismiss, I reassured her that I had it under control. *Besides*, I thought, *I have enough on my plate already—there isn't room for food.*

At which point Jane seemed satisfied, if not completely convinced, and said, "Okay, as long as you're talking to David about this."

Even though David was the only person I fully trusted at the time, I was scared to tell him about my hunger games. Number one, he was a guy, and I didn't think he could relate. More pointedly, he hadn't brought up my weight loss, which allowed me to believe perhaps Jane was overreacting. Most of all, I didn't bring it up with him because I was terrified he would send me away.

A few weeks later, Jane and two other close friends, Jean and Val, staged an intervention during our weekly get-together. Always the first to arrive, I knew something was up when I found Jane already sitting on Jean's family-room couch, coffee mug in hand. They each took a turn sharing their concerns and offering up evidence of my "disordered eating" as if they were reenacting a scene from an ABC Afterschool Special.

Though I knew their hearts were in the right place, I was furious. *They just don't get it,* I thought. *If they did, they wouldn't ask me to eat. They would know how much aliveness there is in hunger—how light and strong it makes me feel. If they got it, they would understand how connected this was to my mom and, more specifically, to not having my mom; in fact, they should applaud me for finding such an elegant outlet for my grief.*

I pleaded, "I'm fine." (*I'm not.*) "Back off." (*Please don't.*) I assured them I had it under control, but I didn't. And, though I couldn't admit it, I was starting to get scared. Every time I reached my stated goal weight, I set a new one before I stepped off the scale. I had reached ninety-nine pounds and was now going for ninety-five, maybe ninety. Yes—ninety sounded better.

My friends gave me an ultimatum: either I would tell David what I was doing or I would go to an eating-disorders clinic within the next week; otherwise, Jane would call David herself. A voice inside me cried out, *Please don't make me eat. Being hungry is all that is feeding me.*

Despite feeling like I was betraying the deepest part of myself, the next week I told David about my friends' intervention because I wanted to avoid the humiliation of Jane's calling him. I also told him how furious I was that they seemed more concerned with what I wasn't eating than with what was eating me. And I cautioned him about wading into this territory—telling him my relationship with food and my body was something I would prefer to protect him from—that food and I have been on rocky terms my whole life. I thought of it like the Middle East—

an untenable, unwinnable conflict. I didn't want him to feel bad if he couldn't help me. And I was quite sure he couldn't.

Thankfully, David didn't freak out. He even understood the aliveness in the hunger, as paradoxical as it sounded, and gave me a beautiful poem on grief by Edna St. Vincent Millay. In it, she expresses her unmitigated disapproval of her loved one's death—which told me David truly understood what I was trying to express via my inelegant and ultimately self-defeating hunger strike. Best of all, he didn't once mention sending me away.

And for the first time in a long time, I felt full.

I wish I could say I went out for a cheeseburger and fries that night. But I didn't. I did, however, start to see what was at stake for me. Not eating was a childlike, fantastical protest. It wasn't about losing weight. It was about losing my mother, my nurturer-in-chief—a role I had unknowingly delegated to her and was refusing for myself.

Feeding myself would mean acknowledging my mother was gone—forever—as in not ever coming back. I wasn't ready. I did not approve. The lost and abandoned child in me was convinced that if I got thin enough, or sick enough, she'd have to come back to feed me. That's what moms do. They feed their children. They don't leave them. Surely she would see how much I still needed her. She wouldn't let me die.

Eventually, though I desperately wanted my mom to save me, it was my commitment to my stepdaughter, Becca, that did. I realized I could continue my hunger strike and starve myself— possibly to death—but not only would doing so not bring my mother back, it would threaten my ability to nurture Becca at a critical time in her young life. I would be a terrible role model for a girl just growing into her own adolescent body. She had already been deeply affected when the mother of one of her closest friends was shipped to an eating-disorders clinic on the other side of the country for three months. If I didn't stop this protest and begin eating (and eventually learn to feed all of my hungers), I would have to leave Becca too. And while my mother was gone, the mothering instinct in me was not.

So I made the first truly nourishing decision of my motherless life and began to eat.

OFFERS HE COULDN'T REFUSE . . .

UNTIL HE DID

Dear David:

I would like to redecorate the Counseling Center entrance, waiting area, and bathroom. My intention is to provide welcoming, comfortable common spaces for your patients and the patients of the other doctors who use these offices.

Why I want to do this:
1. What happens in these offices is sacred and important.

2. It is not unreasonable to imagine that patients enter the building feeling some degree of anxiety and/or distress.

3. Not only does the dismal, run-down decor of the common areas not align with the healing that happens inside these offices, it may actually work against it. I wanted to include, but didn't, "If patients aren't depressed when they enter the building, they will be after spending time in the waiting room."

4. It would bring me a good deal of satisfaction to improve the look and feel of these areas for myself and others.

The work will require nothing from you except answers to the following questions:

1. Do you have any preferred paint colors?

2. Do the books that currently fill the bathtub belong to anyone, or can they be donated?

3. How about the poster of the emaciated and exhausted ballet dancers that is currently hanging in the waiting room?

4. At the very minimum, may I erase the graffiti penciled on the wall of the staircase?

5. What items are necessary in the waiting area?
- *Coat rack?*
- *Seating for how many?*
- *Minimum number of side tables?*
- *Do you need all three trash cans?*

6. Other requirements/parameters?

I will complete the work on a weekend or evening when the offices are not being used and will gladly pay for the renovations.

Guarantee: if you or your colleagues do not like the improvements, I will return the rooms to their original condition and reapply the graffiti.

Most sincerely,
Cheryl

Though David acknowledged the unique and abundant qualifications I would bring to this project, he refused my offer nonetheless. In fact, as I came to discover, David would not accept *any* gift I wanted to give him. These included:

- A book of Mary Oliver poems
- Warm, homemade blueberry muffins in a basket
- A white gardenia (after his eardrum burst)
- Passionate sex in the woods
- A box of honey-peanut Balance Bars, his favorite
- Toe warmers
- An ice-cream cone after he "wrecked" (his word) his knee
- Tickets to a Phillies game
- Beautiful photographs of the Amish countryside to hang in his waiting room
- Passionate sex on the couch in his office
- My kidney, or bone marrow, or any expendable body part

Each time David refuses one of my gifts, my eyes well up with tears and I feel an anguished, desperate combination of rejection and frustration. It is that frustration that fuels my organ-donation fantasy:

- David is sick.
- He needs a kidney in order to survive.
- I rush to the hospital to have my blood drawn to see if I'm a suitable match.
- The next day, his doctor calls and says I am a "perfect match."
- Because he is dying, David has no other choice than to break his rule and accept my kidney.
- Finally, I have something of value to give him.
- Finally, I am able to save his life, the way I feel he is saving mine.

The unsuccessful arguments I make when David refuses me . . . I mean my gifts:

- Caroline, my former therapist, accepted gifts. (Even as I say this, I know I sound like a whiny ten-year-old girl: "But Jessica's parents let her stay up until eleven o'clock." But I can't help myself.)

- Of course I have to give you gifts. It's only human. Don't you want me to be human?

- This lack of reciprocity is untenable. One day you are going to wake up and see my name on your schedule and say to yourself, "Enough. I'm done with this woman. She just takes and takes and takes." You won't say that to me out loud, because you are too kind or loyal or professional, but you will be thinking it, and because I am me, I will feel it, and it will be awful.

- The truth is, I could never give you enough things to pay you back for all you give me, so just humor me and let me sneak in a little token of my affection and appreciation. I promise not to tell anyone.

- This is what I do! This is what I was bred to do. I give. And I'm a great gift-giver. I have a notebook where I track things people tell me they like during the year that I then refer to when it's time to give a birthday or holiday gift. I give good gifts, David. Really, I do. And I never re-gift.

- Who made up these rules, anyway? What if psychologists soon discover that refusing patient gifts is more harmful than helpful? Then what? Can I retroactively give you all these gifts if that should happen?

The good news is, there is nothing I can do to win his esteem and care for me. The bad news is, there is nothing I can do to win his esteem and care for me. And this makes me utterly crazy. In fact, it is unprecedented and somewhat devastating to be with a man I don't have to flatter, fix, or fuck.

MOM, WHERE ARE YOU?

I woke up in a panic. I looked at my clock: 5:23 AM, a full hour before I usually rise. Knowing I hadn't overslept did nothing to calm the sweaty mix of urgency and doom that wrested me from sleep. And it wasn't the first time since my mom had died that this had happened. It was becoming a habit. Two or three times a week, I woke up with an anxious drive to find my mother—the kind of anxious drive that overcame me when I realized my driver's license had fallen out of my pocket while walking in the park, or, worse, the morning Becca's mom called, frantically asking if I had put her on the school bus that day (I had) when the middle school called to alert us that she wasn't in her first-period class. Fortunately, in both instances my dread was quickly replaced with relief when my license and stepdaughter were quickly found safe and whole. I ached for the same relief now, but I knew it would not come to me as swiftly. I had to go looking for it.

Since I had only one appointment later in the day, I decided to go to the cemetery—the last place I had left my mother.

I quickly dressed, fed the cats, gave Gracie her breakfast and a shorter-than-usual walk, and hopped in my car.

It was Thursday, and I knew my father would be at work, so I wouldn't interrupt his daily visit. Even though it was a humid summer day, I felt chilled and slightly queasy as I set foot on the cemetery grounds. It struck me how unprepared I was to visit Mom or anyone here. I never had before. I didn't know what to do or what to say—let alone what to think or feel. I longed for a sign to tell me what the protocols were—what behavior was and was not allowed—like the signs that one sees in parks: Please Don't Feed the Ducks or No Loitering After Dark.

Do I sit or stand? How close to the headstone can I get? Can I touch it? Am I supposed to greet my mother—and the others planted here? Do I talk silently to myself or out loud to her?

Looking down at Mom's shiny marble headstone and imagining her ashes buried beneath the stone, I began feeling claustrophobic on her behalf. Mom hated being in confined, windowless places, which made her decision to have her ashes be buried a bit surprising.

I took a deep breath and began:

"Hi, Mom, it's me, Cheryl. I came here today to find you. I'm not sure I can sleep well again until I do. It only took me forty minutes to get here. There was surprisingly little traffic on the expressway.

"You are resting under a large and lovely maple tree. Do you know that, Mom?

"And do you also know that Dad already purchased his headstone and had it engraved with his name and birthday and placed next to yours? He's counting the days until he joins you. Some days it's like he already has. I wish I knew what to do for him. I can't tell you how many people came up to me at the shivah [the weeklong mourning period in Judaism during which people offer their condolences to the bereaved] and said, 'Take care of your dad.' I'm trying, Mom, I really am. I wish we had talked about this before you died. I wish you could have told me how to deal with his sorrow. It seems like he's trying to be more in your world than mine. I am starting to feel like I lost you both—you to cancer and Dad to grief."

This definitely wasn't helping. I had come here trying to quell my sorrow for one parent, and now I was longing for two of them. This couldn't be good. This was not why people come to cemeteries. Don't they come to feel connected to their loved ones? To commune with them in some way? To leave feeling comforted? Or maybe they come out of duty. I really don't know.

"Okay, this isn't working for me, Mom. I'm sorry. I'm sorry you are here, and I'm sorry you are not here. I'm sorry that despite ten years of Hebrew school, I don't have strong enough clarity or faith to know for sure where you are. And I'm deeply sorry for feeling this, Mom, but I'm sorry you died before Dad.

"I will keep looking for you. I'm leaving now. Good-bye, Mom."

As I walked back to my car, a part of me knew I was engaged in magical thinking and a part of me didn't.

⚜

A week later, I imagined Mom might be feeling nostalgic, since I certainly was, so I decided to look for her in the house I grew up in. I didn't know the young couple who currently lived in the house, so I asked my childhood next-door neighbors to broker a brief visit.

Gingerly, I pulled up to the curb in front of the house. My parents moved into this two-story, three-bedroom home with moss-green siding and black shutters in 1963 and left it thirty-three years later. I still remember the phone call from my father announcing the move. The first thing I asked when I heard his voice was, "What happened to Mom?" as it was unusual for him to call me. My father hated talking on the phone. He would only grudgingly hold one to his ear when Mom called me at college, and after a few minutes he would find a reason to get off, saying, "Mom will catch me up later." So hearing only his voice on the line scared me. But he quickly assured me Mom was okay and said he had big news to share: "Mom and I bought a new home and are moving at the end of the month. You need to come over this weekend and get your stuff from the attic."

Now I was doubly shocked. Not only was my dad calling me, but he was telling me he was selling the house I grew up in—the house he had sworn he would die in. Had he fallen and hit his head?

Turns out he *had* fallen—fallen in love with a new home twenty minutes away from where they now lived. The house itself was small, he said, but elegantly designed and nestled on over an acre of land. Every room had doors or windows leading to a lawn or garden. "It is the house Mom deserves," he crowed, and he wanted to give it to her. Just like that.

Back at my childhood home, the first thing I noticed when I stepped out of the car was how much smaller the yard looked than it felt to me as a child. And what had been a gentle slope of lush green was now a flattened slab of brownish grass. I took a deep breath. *At least it's easier to mow*, I thought.

As I walked up the driveway, I noticed the familiar black-and-gold mailbox hanging next to the front door and recalled Ed, our mailman, who often left lollipops or dog treats along with the mail.

The current homeowners greeted me politely, though cautiously. I nervously stammered out a hello and offered the wife a bouquet of daisies and a pink baby blanket for their infant daughter.

Being inside the house felt simultaneously familiar and deeply foreign. And it tipped toward feeling completely awkward when the wife offered to show me around, as if I hadn't spent eighteen years of my life there. *Shouldn't I be showing her around?* I thought. *Or, more to the point of my visit, shouldn't Mom come bounding down the stairs to welcome us both?* And in the absence of her ethereal appearance, wasn't I obligated to tell these interlopers what had happened within these walls?

Sharing a memory or two felt all the more pressing once the tour began and I started seeing remnants from my childhood that were still in place—like the old-fashioned telephone hung in the middle of the upstairs hallway. The phone had an extralong cord so it could reach into my brother's room and mine. And there were dozens of my parents' hardback books still on the custom-made bookshelves in what had been my brother's room. Even more startling was seeing my always-one-shade-or-another-of-pink bedroom awash in blood-red paint and adorned with World Wrestling Entertainment posters. I decided not to challenge their decorating taste by telling them about the Scott Baio and Donny Osmond posters that used to adorn the same walls.

As the wife continued escorting me through the home, I couldn't help but notice the stained carpets, peeling wallpaper, and uncovered light fixtures. The only positive improvement was a linoleum floor that replaced the blue kitchen carpet my parents had installed in the kitchen. When we walked through that room, I could almost smell the Mrs. Paul's fish sticks Mom would bake on nights my dad wasn't home for dinner. And for a moment I thought I heard the Ella Fitzgerald tape she sang along to when she was in an especially good mood. But then I realized this too was magical thinking. There were no true signs of my mother here.

From the kitchen window, I could see the backyard garden that my father took so much pride in. Now it was overgrown and undernourished. Even the willow tree we buried my dog's ashes under seemed weary and in need of something.

It was then I grasped I would never find my mother here. Which was actually a relief, because if she had been here she would have wept, along with the willow tree, at the decorating choices the new family had made.

Part of me wanted to ask for a few moments of unaccompanied time in the house, but I noticed the husband looking at his watch. Before I left, there was one last thing I felt compelled to do, so I hastily dug into my purse and pulled out a picture of Mom laughing on a chair in the backyard. She must have been about forty at the time.

"I just want to show you a picture of my mother. Her name was Wendy. She loved everything about this house. She especially loved the light that streamed into the kitchen in the morning and the sun as it streamed into the living room at dusk. She made it our home. And she died this past April."

When the couple nodded politely yet refrained from asking any questions, I thanked them for their time and left.

As soon as I drove away, I started crying and pulled over to the side of the road. When I turned on the radio in an effort to gain my composure, I heard the tail end of a newly released country song. The song was "The House That Built Me." In it Miranda Lambert croons, "I thought if I could touch this place or feel it, this brokenness inside me might start healing."

❦

Despite being zero for two on my search for Mom, I remained undaunted and quickly decided my next visit would be to the home she shared with my father. In fact, I chastised myself for not having started my search there—after all, it was the last place she called home and the place she most loved being. Maybe she hadn't left yet.

So the next weekend I asked my dad if I could come over to the house. He was more than happy to have me visit, as he wanted to show me some changes he had made—things he thought Mom would like.

When I arrived, he met me at the car and escorted me into the garage. He had commissioned a local artist to paint flowers and fruits of various colors on the storage cabinets that lined the garage walls. Next, he took me into the kitchen and pointed out new folk-art paintings, place mats, and a fruit bowl. He seemed quite pleased with himself and was most excited about showing me Mom's newly repurposed office. Though I was impressed and proud of his initiative, I was a little taken aback at how quickly he had cleaned it out and turned it into a reading room, and I wondered if I would find Mom at all now that he had made all these changes.

After my father finished his tour, I asked if I could go upstairs into Mom's bedroom by myself (Dad had moved his bedroom to the first floor since a foot injury had made climbing stairs difficult). He said that was fine and told me to take as long as I wanted.

I ascended the plush beige-carpeted steps that led to her bedroom, not knowing quite what I would find or feel when I arrived. The first thing I noticed was how beautiful a room it was. It had a skylight above the king-size bed and sliding glass doors that opened to a large balcony overlooking the lawn and gardens—the very same gardens Alan and I had been married in a little more than three years earlier. And this was the bedroom I had readied myself in then. Who knew I'd be in this room again, so soon, also trying to ready myself? The room felt light and peaceful and remained untouched—as if Mom had climbed out of bed just this morning. The white-lacquer headboard was still filled with books; a pair of her glasses rested on the bedside table, along with more books. When I sat on the edge of the bed, I could even smell her Jo Malone Amber & Lavender perfume lingering on the sheets.

While I sat on the bed, I recalled the last time Mom was in it. I knew exactly when it was, because I was in it too. It was a Sunday at 8:00 AM, about a month before she died. Mom had been discharged from the nursing home a few days earlier. The plan had been for her to come home and, with Dad's help, my visits, and some in-home nursing care, get strong enough to start a second round of chemotherapy. But Dad had been nervous about the plan from the start, and it was more difficult than any of us had realized to keep her comfortable, keep up with her medicines, and move her in and out of chairs and beds.

The defining event happened on a Saturday night, when Mom fell out of bed while trying to get to the bathroom. Dad did not hear her calling. She lay on the floor for hours, until he woke up the next morning and went to check on her. My father called me at 6:00 AM in tears, saying he couldn't take care of her at home. It was too much. We needed to take Mom back to the nursing home, but he couldn't tell her himself. He didn't want to disappoint her or break her heart (though it was his heart that was breaking). Would I please come over and tell her?

I immediately drove to their home and found Dad scared and exhausted in his study. I hugged him and told him he had done his best and that I would talk with Mom. She would understand.

When I entered Mom's bedroom, she was sleeping and curled up like a child in bed. And now that the cancer had spread to her brain, her mental capacities were rendering her more childlike every day. Her face was swollen from tears and the steroids she was on; her eyes were moist and tired. I climbed into the bed and cuddled up next to her, gathering my thoughts, praying I could find the right words.

When she woke up, I asked, "How are you doing, Mom? Dad said you took a spill."

She tried to laugh it off, but I could tell she was shaken. We wouldn't know for another day that she had severely bruised two ribs and sprained her wrist. I gently began stroking her arm.

"Mom," I said, "you've been through a lot already. Do you still want to fight? Still want to go through more treatment? You don't have to, you know. You can stop if you want."

"Yes. Yes, honey, I do. I'm not ready to be done. I have so much to live for."

"Well, then you need to get stronger so your body can absorb more treatment. And you're not able to get stronger at home. Dad can't take care of you the way he wants to and the way you need. You need more care than we can give you here. So if you still want to fight, we need to take you back to the nursing home."

"I don't want to be a burden to Dad."

"Mom, you're not a burden to Dad. His heart is breaking. He wants you here with him, of course, but he also wants you safe and well. We all do."

"Do you think I can get back into the same room I had before? And do you think Natalie can be my nurse again?"

"I think we can try, Mom. We can try."

"Okay. Will I be disappointing Dad?" She started to cry.

"No, Mom, you could never disappoint Dad. He is so proud of you. *I* am so proud of you, Mom. I love you so much."

"Okay. Then I'm ready. I'll go back to the nursing home. I'll get strong. I'll get more treatment. I'll beat this cancer."

"I know you will, Mom."

❧

I sat on the edge of her bed, recalling that conversation. Tears welled in my eyes. Despite the optimism I conveyed to her that day, I knew in my heart that she wouldn't be coming back to this house. And I knew now, as I sat on the bed, that she still hadn't come back. Mom wasn't here. I was just visiting some of her things and some of my memories—not her. I stood up, descended the steps, thanked my dad for letting me come by, and left.

Clearly, I was not going to find Mom in the obvious places. I had to look elsewhere.

One of my mom's close friends believed Mom came to her as a bird. So I started paying attention to the birds around my house and on my walks, hoping one of them would distinguish itself—maybe a woodpecker would begin tapping out a message in Morse code, or a songbird would start singing "I'll Never Fall in Love Again," one of Mom's favorites. It didn't happen.

Then I wondered if Mom would use Gracie to get a message to me. She knew how connected Gracie and I were and how much time we spent together. It could happen.

So I asked, "Gracie, do you have anything special you want to say to me? Anything on your mind?"

She cocked her head to the left.

Nothing.

A dog she was. A messenger she wasn't.

It was time for a spiritual intervention. I knew precious little about the Jewish perspective on the afterlife. In fact, I was much better versed in, though much more dubious about, what Catholicism had to say on the matter. I learned this from the O'Connors, who regularly celebrated, rather than mourned, the deaths of their loved ones. After all, they proclaimed, the deceased person was now with Jesus in heaven. Time to rejoice. This philosophy seemed like a "fast pass" to the front of the grieving line. Just as you can buy a FastPass to rides at Disney World so you don't have to wait two hours in line, and can just skip the hard part and enjoy the ride, how great to bypass the hell that is grief and go directly to party time.

I called my rabbi and asked if he would meet me so I could learn where Jews believed Mom was now. When we sat down for lunch, I got right to the point.

"Thank you for meeting with me, Rabbi. I am especially grateful since, as you know, I only went to services twice last year."

He assured me this was a common occurrence and acknowledged that death can be difficult.

Well, that's the understatement of a lifetime, I thought, before replying, "Yes, it can. And I need to caution you that I might tear up during our meal. And I want to apologize for not being better versed in Jewish beliefs about the afterlife."

"Cheryl, I'm not afraid of your tears, and you shouldn't be either. You are brave and wise to be asking such questions."

"I don't feel brave, Rabbi. I feel bereft. And I feel my mom is lost to me. I want to find her. Please tell me where she is."

The rabbi gently explained that, according to Jewish teachings, for the first year after a loved one dies, her or his soul is on a journey to "the world to come" (*olam ha'ba*). I could contribute to my mom's peaceful journey by thinking of her every day.

I was grateful for his kindness but resisted the urge to ask him if he truly believed this stuff and instead asked for the check.

⁙

For months after she died, Mom didn't feel gone to me—she felt lost. Perhaps this was what others felt too when they said or wrote in their condolence cards, "I'm sorry for your loss." I wasn't just missing Mom; *Mom was missing*, and I had to find her. Finding her seemed like the surest way of finding me again too. But I had looked everywhere and I hadn't found her. My meeting with the rabbi confirmed that while there was something I could do to assist Mom in her cosmic journey, it was clearly a journey away from me. The awful truth is that we were indeed in two different worlds. Mom wasn't lost after all. She was gone. And if I had any hope of finding her, I had to stay still long enough to grieve the truth of that. I had to stop racing from place to place like a lost puppy. I had to look within.

I CAN'T HEAR YOU

As soon as I saw the number flash on my ringing cell phone, I recognized it as David's and knew something was wrong. It was 8:40 in the morning. I was counting the hours (just six more to go) until our appointment that afternoon. I really needed to see him and had already chosen my outfit: a short khaki skirt with a J.Crew orange and cream–striped top. The top's boatneck made my collarbones stick out in a good way.

Why was David calling me now? If he had just needed to change our meeting time, he would have sent me an email. This couldn't be good.

Afraid of what he would say, I let the call go to voice mail, wanting to delay the inevitable. (And the thought of having his recorded message on my phone so I could hear his voice on demand *was* quite appealing.)

I waited a full hour before listening to his message, hoping that doing so would make the anticipated bad news good. Maybe he wanted to see me earlier in the day and I wouldn't have to wait six hours. Or maybe he had decided that since I was such a frequent visitor, he would give me a discount or a T-shirt or a coffee mug with his face on it. Maybe . . .

Finally I dialed my phone and listened to his message:

"Hi, Cheryl. David here. Look, I'm sorry for the short notice, but my eardrum burst. I'm in a doctor's office, waiting for treatment. I'll be okay, but I won't be able to see you this afternoon and I'll have to let you know about Friday. I realize it's hard for you to miss our session and hard for you to know I'm in pain. This might be a good time to journal. Maybe we can do a short check-in by phone in a few days. I'll be in touch."

I listened to the message two more times to make sure I hadn't missed anything. He sounded weary and maybe even a bit concerned. This was not good. My palms were sweating. A bowling ball had lodged itself in my stomach. *David is in pain. It must be my fault. It's my fault his eardrum burst. All the time he spends listening to me—his poor, adorable ear just couldn't take it anymore.* "Enough already," *it said.* "I'm outta here." *(Or is it* "outta hear"?*)*

I have to do something. But what? I know! I'll start investigating homeopathic treatments on the web. Surely no one else has thought to do that yet. I'll send him a list this afternoon. I'll take care of him.

And as I was investigating alternative treatments, I couldn't help think how fucking ironic—a therapist with a burst eardrum.

Then I cried for both of us.

THEY DID THE BEST THEY COULD

"I came here to feel better. I came here to figure out how to get Peter to take me back. I didn't come here to talk about my childhood," I sobbed to Caroline. "Besides, I told you, my parents did the best they could."

I was twenty-three, drowning in a puddle of unworthiness and despair because of my recent breakup, and had started therapy with Caroline in an attempt to stop hurting.

"Cheryl, sometimes the path to feeling better involves feeling worse for a bit. And let me remind you again: I'm not here to help you get Peter back. None of us can make someone love us. I'm here to help you find out why you feel so worthless without him."

For years, when reflecting on my childhood difficulties, I reflexively told myself my parents did the best they could. It was a mantra for me and a get-out-of-jail-free card for them. Any and all less-than-perfect memories were locked up tight; picture an eight-by-eight-foot steel vault with the words THEY DID THE BEST THEY COULD painted in black letters across it, and me, dressed in a navy blue security guard's uniform, standing in front, making sure no one dared enter—especially me!

Caroline continued, "Cheryl, you have told me you had an ideal childhood, you have placed your father on a pedestal and speak glowingly of your mother, yet you have also acknowledged how sad and lonely you felt as a child, and how you suffered from crippling separation anxiety, similar to the suffering you are experiencing now with Peter. I'm wondering how your parents, however well-meaning, may have contributed to your sadness and anxiety."

"I was just an overly sensitive child," I assured her. "My parents did the best they could. Really they did."

The truth was, I wasn't ready to step inside the vault. Though I didn't know exactly what demons lurked inside, I had an inkling that they were best kept hidden.

Years later, when I began therapy with David, ostensibly to help grieve my mother, I told him too that there was no need to poke around my childhood. Yes, there was a vault—I discovered it with Caroline—but we didn't need to open it. I had long since forgiven my parents for any unintended failings. And now was not the time. After all, my mother had died and couldn't even defend herself, and my father was in such a fragile state, how could I, and why would I, open the vault, especially if it meant casting them as anything less than noble? After all, I assured him, they did the best they could.

Yet as I began experiencing my grief, examining my contribution to the frail state of my marriage, considering the reasons I had not had a child of my own, and noticing just how difficult eye contact and receiving comfort from others was for me, I began to see that while my struggles may not have been born by design, they didn't arise by accident either. I came by them honestly. And finding the freedom and wholeness I now yearned for required me to do more than just acknowledge the vault. I had to open it up.

The first thing that came tumbling out was this hymn, by Franklin E. Belden:

If any little word of mine
May make a life the brighter;
If any little song of mine
May make a heart the lighter,
God help me speak the little word,
And take my bit of singing
And drop it in some lonely vale,
To set the echoes ringing.

If any little love of mine
May make a life the sweeter;
If any little care of mine
May make a friend's the fleeter;
If any lift of mine may ease
The burden of another,
God give me love, and care, and strength,
To help my toiling brother.

I read this at my brother's bar mitzvah when I was fourteen years old. And these words were more than poetic for me—they were prescriptive. I was born and bred to be kind, sensitive, accommodating, and selfless. Being so was part of the implicit contract I had with my parents. My sensitivity and kindness was an extension of them. It made them feel good about themselves, perhaps even more than it made them feel good about me. And it felt vital to have them feel good. It was the currency between us: in exchange for being sensitive, solicitous, and kind, I could stay. Their approval, if not their love, was the ticket to their warm home, their healthy meals, the perks of an uppermiddle-class life.

"What's wrong with being kind and solicitous?" I asked David defensively when I read him the poem. "Aren't these virtues? Besides, they served me quite well at home, school, and camp. Not only that, but through them I developed an exquisitely sensitive antenna for intuiting other people's feelings and desires—one that I use both professionally and personally even now."

"There is nothing wrong with those virtues. In fact, your so-called antenna didn't just serve you—I think it saved you. It was a brilliant skill, and you were deft at executing it. I just wonder if it also cost you."

"Well, anything it cost me paled in comparison with what it gave my parents. My dad had already endured so much *unkindness* in his childhood. Do you know he used to lie in bed and ask God to take his life during the night so he wouldn't have to hear his parents' violent fights and endure their neglect and abuse of him and his brother? Wasn't it my duty to at least try to make up for that?"

"No, Cheryl. Actually, it wasn't," David replied quietly.

When I reflected on David's response, it suddenly hit me: kindness wasn't just one play in the playbook—it was the only game in town. And the exquisitely sensitive antenna that allowed me to read other people didn't pick up any signals when I tuned in to my own experience. Perhaps this explains why I had no way of knowing when I felt angry, lonely, sad, or frustrated. When I tried adjusting the antenna, all I heard was static, followed by the all-too-clear commercial interruption *They did the best they could.*

With David's patient prodding and gentle wrangling, I continued further into the vault and found myself more surprised by what was missing from my childhood than by what was actually there.

MESS

Both of my parents delighted in making our home a place of beauty, function, and organization. Beauty wasn't an afterthought, it was a tonic—especially for my father, who could not tolerate, and went to great lengths to avoid, mess in any form. One would think raising children and having a no-mess policy would be incompatible goals, but if you are the parent, you set the policy. And if the policy doesn't change, the child does.

Everything (and everyone) in our home had a place and had to be in it at all times. It was not okay to leave a dish in the sink or a bed unmade. The upside was that we lived in the largest, loveliest house on our block. So lovely that Mary Beth McBride, my friend from across the street, once confessed that she occasionally asked her friends to drop her off at our home and pretended it was hers. And it was common for my parents to meet me at the front door when I came home from college and lead me to their latest artistic acquisition before I even had time to put down my laundry basket and backpack.

The following is a poem I found in a journal I kept as a child. I was eleven years old when I wrote it.

MOTHER KNOWS BEST   December 1, 1975
Her mother told her to
keep her room neat
Her mother told her to
always wipe her feet.
Her mother told her to
say Thank you & please, and try not to sneeze.
Her mother told her this & that
Her mother told her not to get fat
And now I know a girl who keeps
her room neat and always wipes her
feet. I know a girl
that says thank you & please and never
tries to sneeze.
I know a girl who does this and that
And certainly is not fat.

But really, growing up in a meticulously clean and lovely house was worth the price, right? And beauty in its many forms is now something I also take great comfort in. Isn't that a gift?

PLAY

Play is messy. So if there are to be no messes, then there isn't much play. While my father played brilliantly with words for a living, he couldn't figure out how to play with me. Besides, play represented everything he could not abide. Play was spontaneous, not always pretty, vulnerable, silly, and pointless (but not purposeless, as I learned much later.) My mother was innately playful—she enjoyed singing, dancing, and playing piano—but when she did these things, my father squirmed or left the room altogether. I quickly picked up on his discomfort and came to believe that spontaneous expressions of joy—especially about something or someone other than my father—were an act of disloyalty and could result in shame or even emotional exile. Though I do remember playing quietly with my dolls in my room and staging plays with kids on the street, my father was never involved. Note to childhood self: don't sing or dance or frolic.

In her own way, my mother also discouraged my play. I remember how she enjoyed having me sit on her lap or stand by her side when the moms gathered on the curb to chat while the other kids on our street played kickball. (I think one of the reasons I enjoy facilitating women's groups is that I spent so much time listening to women talk amongst themselves as a child.)

"Still," I protested to David, "not playing is really no big deal. Right? I did so many other things as a kid. I wrote poetry, went to summer camp—which was really one giant playground—and got to work at Burger King when I turned fifteen. That was pretty cool. Maybe I've just forgotten the times my parents played with me, since I do recall my father playing catch with my brother."

David reminded me of the panic and jealousy that erupt in me when I watch Alan, Andrew, and Becca roughhouse on the floor or frolic in the ocean. It is sometimes all I can do not to run away, and joining in feels out of the question.

PHYSICAL CONTACT

While my mother was physically affectionate to the point of being overwhelming—often insisting I kiss her on the lips and hug her long and hard—my father seemed to have an invisible electric fence wired around him at all times. If I got too close, I risked electrocuting us both. I remember being stunned during my brother's wedding rehearsal when my father momentarily draped his arm around my shoulder. I'm thankful that someone snapped a picture of it; otherwise, I would not believe it happened. I have no memories of finding shelter in his lap, running into his arms, or even holding his hand. In fact, when we would go on errands together, he would walk so fast I would have to run to keep up with him, for fear of being left behind. To this day, Becca threatens to sign me up for a speed-walking race if I don't slow down when we are in the mall, and Alan gets especially annoyed when I walk too fast for him to comfortably hold my hand.

But how can I blame my parents? My mom, being so young and homesick for her parents when I was a baby, must have been starved for affection, and my dad, who worked days and nights, had no experience giving or receiving it. And even though holding Alan still requires a bit of thought, at least I am able to be affectionate to my kids, pets, and friends. My ambivalence regarding giving and receiving affection is *my* problem now. My parents certainly did the best they could.

TRAFFIC, CROWDS, AND WAITING

We arrived at performances thirty minutes before the curtains opened and usually sat in the back row, with my dad occupying the aisle seat. We left at or before the final curtain call. When we attended baseball games, which we did three or four times every summer, we were at the ballpark when the gates opened and left during the seventh-inning stretch. My brother and I joke that we never realized until we were adults that a ballgame lasted nine innings.

And an upscale restaurant felt more like a fast-food chain as my father asked the waitress to take our order within a minute of handing us our menus. Despite my mother's pleading to "take it slow," he would request the check as we were swallowing our last bite of dinner and would glower at my mother if she asked for a cup of coffee after the meal.Today, I have to consciously force myself to slow down or not rush our server or my family when we dine at a restaurant. Still, who could blame him? My father was a busy man. He always had papers to grade or commercials to write. And if he hadn't done these things, we wouldn't have had nice meals out in restaurants anyway.

CONFLICT (A LOT OF SIGHS)

Conflict—even mild disagreement or the expression of a "negative" emotion, especially anger—was not okay. And who could blame my dad? He had had enough rage and ruckus as a child to last a lifetime. His capacity for more had expired. (I suppose this explains my penchant for and adeptness at mediating family conflict now. We laugh when two people in my family are disagreeing and I step in. Someone asks me, "Whose side are you on?" and I say, "Everybody's.") But while my father rarely expressed his displeasure overtly, he often expressed it through sighs. He had an entire vocabulary of sighs. And with my exquisitely attuned antenna, I served an important role as chief sigh-interpreter and loyal discomfort-reducer by jumping into action when I heard them.

There was the Wendy-you-are-embarrassing-me sigh that he paired with an eye roll when we were in public and Mom struck up a conversation with a stranger, at which point I would lightly touch Mom's arm and lead her away.

He used his I'm-ready-to-go-home-now sigh when we were at family gatherings. He'd let this one out about twenty minutes after we arrived and usually a good hour and a half before my mom was ready to leave. When I heard this sigh, I would come to the corner of the room he had sequestered himself in to keep him company.

There was the let's-end-this-meal-now sigh, used to indicate that he wanted to get up from the dinner table and go into his den to read, at which point I would gobble up the last bits of food on my plate and say something like, "Thanks, Mom. I'm stuffed. Your meatloaf was really good tonight."

And, of course, there was the you're-not-really-going-to-eat-that sigh when I dared to ask for dessert or open the refrigerator between meals. Eventually I learned to cough when I opened the refrigerator door so my dad wouldn't hear it squeak.

And I heard him sigh most deeply when he plodded up the stairs to his bedroom after returning home late from work. It was as if he were scaling Everest with rocks in his pockets—not so much out of breath as out of life energy.

"But of course he was out of life energy," I told David. "The man was always battling one or more chronic infirmities and had to work for everything he had and everything we had. For all the agony it caused me, my brother and I had summer camps and good health care, eight presents exquisitely wrapped for Hanukkah every year, our first cars and college educations paid for, Phillies games, piano lessons, and even, after we wore my dad down when I was fifteen years old, a loyal and lovable boxer named Tonto.

"And we had all of this because my dad, coming from nothing, made himself quite something—a beloved professor and successful and admired advertising executive. And we had it because my mom stayed home with my brother and me when we were young and then took jobs outside the home to help support us. And most of all, we had it because we were loved. As best they could, my parents loved us."

And David calmly replied, "Yes, Cheryl. That is all true. And it's also true that your parents weren't able to give you some important things that you needed, and it cost you then and it's costing you now."

ME!

When I look back at what it was like to live in the be-kind-make-no-mess world of my childhood, I see my young self tucked tightly into a straitjacket of neatness, kindness, and pleasing. There was no room for hunger of any kind, no room for anger, for joy, for play, for "me."

The vault of my childhood memories contains so many absences that I had to look deeper, to find and acknowledge what *was* present.

FEAR

While there was no room in my childhood for me, there was plenty of room for fear and shame. I was terrified of making a mess (though I often felt like one) and of being the straw that broke my father's fragile back. I was afraid of being rejected, afraid of being fat, afraid of a boy's or a man's attention, afraid of leaving home, afraid to be at home. Most of all, I was afraid of not being enough—and, consequently, not being loved.

And as I chronicled for David all that was and was not inside the vault, and began to put aside my excuses for my parents' behavior, I realized with some degree of horror that while my parents didn't overtly abuse me as a child, they did *ab*normally *use* me.

My mother used me to protect herself and suffocated me with her needs, then sent me to school and camp without the social and emotional support I needed to succeed. She also, to my knowledge, never insisted Dad get professional help for the depression and social anxiety that plagued him and held all of us hostage. Maybe it was because, as she unabashedly told Mark and me, she loved him most of all.

My father used me as his buffer against discomfort. Though he joked I was his favorite daughter, even though I was his only daughter, I still felt my status was conditional. I was competing with his young, pretty female students—constantly auditioning to be his number-one groupie. Keeping him safe. Defending him. Adoring him. Staying loyal. Yet it was a one-sided deal. Though I was desperate to get his affection and attention, I blamed myself when I could not and concluded that I was unlovable. I desperately wanted to heal his pain—to make up for his notoriously hidden yet hideous childhood. When I became a wife and stepmom, I felt the same way I did then—as if I had to make up for all the pain that came before me. Not only did I feel it was my job to make up for it, I actually felt like it was my fault to begin with! I was beginning to understand the extent to which and the reasons why I lived my life as an apology.

With David's help, I learned that protecting my parents when I was a child saved me. But now protecting them was hurting me. For me to genuinely forgive them, I had to acknowledge that their actions and inactions hurt me—in the same way in which, when someone accidentally steps on my toe, it doesn't mean my toe doesn't ache, and it doesn't mean I have to say, "It's fine," instead of "Ouch!"

So yes—my parents did the best they could. And it just so happens that it wasn't good enough to give me the gift of worthiness and "enoughness" that I needed. It wasn't fine. It hurt then and it hurts now.

Ouch.

EMBEDDED

I never expected to start the new year in a Sleepy's Mattress store, telling Alan that we can't choose a mattress based on price alone. We have to lie down on each one and see what feels comfortable, what feels right.

I didn't expect we'd be ready to invest in a new mattress now. What I really mean is, I never expected to be ready to re-invest in my marriage. One year ago, I was wondering where I'd be sleeping if I left both our marriage and our bed. And now we're discussing the merits of foam versus springs with Lee the mattress guy.

To say that my first few years of marriage were difficult and disillusioning is an understatement. In retrospect, how could they have been anything else? I had to merge forty years of single life into a marriage with a man, his two children, and his fiercely involved ex-wife—not to mention becoming a homeowner in a new town and then coping with my mother's unexpected illness and death.

Additionally, I had rented a one-bedroom apartment four miles from our home to house my two cats and serve as my office, since my stepson has cat allergies. Though it was a necessary sacrifice, it didn't stop me from feeling a wretched sense of guilt and longing when I left the cats to fend for themselves every evening.

But it wasn't just the enormity of the changes that were difficult, I was also striving to live up to unconscious standards of how I thought a wife and stepmom should behave. Immediately and without question I assumed virtually all the responsibility for the domestic aspects of our lives: doing everyone's laundry, getting the kids ready and taking them to school so Alan could get to the gym before work, and planning and making healthy dinners that I had never cooked before, all while trying to keep my own career afloat.

The same instincts for healing and helping Alan that had pervaded our courtship jumped into overdrive when I became his wife. I thought it was essential for me to make his life as comfortable as possible and to put his needs and the kids' needs before mine. After all, I told myself, they had suffered so much already; I didn't want to cause them any additional pain. My life felt like a perpetual audition—or an episode of *Survivor*. I was afraid that one wrong move (or, God forbid, a burp or fart) would get me voted off the family.

So, while Alan's life pretty much went back to normal after we married, mine was turned upside down and inside out—like the laundry that had felt so sexy to do before (had I really thought that?)—and slowly began feeling quite onerous.

Which is exactly how I began feeling about sex. The sex that had been so feral and urgent when Alan and I were courting became, almost overnight, another chore. And I felt horrible about it. Alan was as good-looking and in shape as ever. I used to dream about having a man want me as much as he did, but now, instead of feeling wanted, I felt burdened. I had somehow traded desire for duty. I never said no to Alan—I believed it was an essential part of my job description. I recalled numerous conversations I'd had over the years with male colleagues who opined about the sex they were no longer getting from their wives. At the time, I'd thought, *Oh, how awful—how could a wife not want to make love to her husband?* Now, I got it.

After *decades* of fantasizing about true love, I never expected marriage to be so hard. I never expected the love songs to lie. I never expected to be at least half of the problem, or to realize that the intimacy I most wanted from Alan was what I most feared having. I never expected that buying a king-size mattress would require king-size courage.

A king-size bed for a king-size marriage. If we could be comfortable in a new bed, could we be comfortable in our lives together?

After we had moved into our home, we had made every room functional and beautiful. Every room except our bedroom—why didn't we *start* with our bedroom? Our bed? Why didn't I insist on it? Such neglect. Taking something so new and precious for granted—despite the statistics. Crazy.

Instead, I learned to leap onto a very-high-off-the-ground queen-size bed inherited from Alan's first marriage. The bed was half as high and half as old as I was. And I learned how not to bump into two of the four posts that punctuated the ends of the bed, often imagining them as spears when insomnia relegated them to nighttime shadows. And this was before Alan's snoring became not so cute anymore, and before my slow retreat inward after my mother died.

What is it to be embedded, not just wedded, with another person the way one is with a husband? I never imagined I'd miss my single-girl days, when I slept undisturbed with my cats, Thai curled at my feet, and Mystic nestled under my chin. So much easier sleeping with cats than with a husband.

When I first brought up the idea of graduating from a queen- to a king-size mattress, Alan said he thought that was one step toward a divorce. I told him it was actually one giant step (at least for me) away from divorce.

Back at the mattress store, Lee is explaining motion control. He says it will prevent me from waking up when Alan bounces into bed after a Phillies win. I wonder if a lack of turbulence in our bed would create less turbulence out of it. Would a peaceful night of rest translate into a peaceful day of marriage?

Lee is telling us about the twenty-year warranty. Twenty years! Is that for the bed or for the marriage? If the marriage doesn't last twenty more years, can I return the mattress?

And now he's talking about a comfort guarantee. Yes. I'll take it. I want a comfort guarantee, because for most of these five years, I've been uncomfortable. And if buying a mattress from Lee the mattress guy can guarantee my comfort, sign me up. *Now.*

I want my mattress to be perfect. No lumps. No noise. No squeaks. I want it to be welcoming, calming, and soothing, a foundation for only good dreams, and a sanctuary from the aches and pains of life. It's what I want my marriage to be, too.

So Alan and I bought the king-size, supercomfy, low-turbulence, high-priced mattress *and* the matching pad. As Alan completed the paperwork, it occurred to me that we were spending more money on bedding than we had on couples' counseling this past year, yet doing so felt oddly therapeutic. And, come to think of it, Lee the mattress guy, his voice as soft as down, did facilitate our mattress choice with more ease than we usually muster trying to agree on a Saturday-night movie.

As we left the store, feeling more optimistic than when we had entered, Alan reached for my hand. And it suddenly dawned on me that changing the bed, instead of the person lying in it with you, even when life gets lumpy, may be exactly what being embedded is about. Or so I hoped.

COUCH SURFING

I don't know if it was the compassion in her eyes when she asked, or the fact that she charged $210 an hour and I didn't want to waste a minute, but I took a deep breath and dove in.

"I'm in love with David. And it's killing me." Before I could say another word, I began to cry. Not just tear up, as I often did in front of David, but really cry. It was as if all of the tears that had been held prisoner for so long had finally been paroled and came dashing out unbidden. They were tears of shame—falling for another unavailable man—tears of loneliness, and tears of grief.

"It's okay, Cheryl. It's okay to cry. Take your time. I'm right here."

I was sitting on another couch with another psychologist sitting across from me. But instead of being on the third floor of a converted Victorian house, I was on the first floor of a sterile stucco professional building. And instead of decorating the space in my mind, struggling to avoid eye contact and unbridled lust, I was sinking deeper into the couch, admiring the brown speckled frames of her eyeglasses and wondering if she had ever longed for a man she couldn't have.

At David's suggestion, I had scheduled this consultation to discuss my mounting distress about my mounting crush on him. He thought speaking to another professional might give me some perspective on my experience. When he first brought it up, I panicked, thinking he was trying to pawn me off on someone else (I wouldn't have blamed him), though he assured me he wasn't.

I felt humiliated being there—like I had been sent to the principal's office for bad behavior. But I was desperate. My feelings for David were not like any crush I'd had before. It wasn't like spending hours looking at Mr. 11's picture in my high school yearbook, or going to sleep looking up at the photos of Scott Baio plastered on my bedroom ceiling, or even the giddy feeling I got from stealing glances with the shortstop in my college cafeteria. It was not pleasant. It was not fun or fanciful. I thought this crush was going to kill me. I wanted to know if this was normal—if I was normal—and if my therapy sessions were doing more harm than good. I was still deeply homesick for my mother and wondered if I was making any progress at all.

Thankfully, the psychologist was a woman. And she had warm eyes and a soft voice. She spoke slowly, sometimes haltingly. I could have melted inside her pauses. No doubt many of her patients did.

When I composed myself, she asked me to elaborate on my experience with David.

I reached into my purse and retrieved the note I had brought in anticipation of her question—wanting, of course, to be prepared and articulate just in case the tears escaped and I lost my way. I began to read:

"When I'm not with him, I'm miserable. I think about him all the time. I wonder what he is doing and wish I could be with him. I count the hours until our next session, imagining that when I'm there I'll feel better and more comfortable, but I never do. I arrive nervous. I worry if I'm a moment late (which I never am), have a hair out of place, cry, eat, forget to bring a check, or run out of prepared things to say, my standing with him will suffer and he'll fire me. There is little or no margin for error, for mess, for *me*.

"At the start of each session, I try to discern how David is doing that day so I can determine what to do, however subtle or slight, to accommodate him, or certainly not add to any of his discomfort.

"Each session I struggle to manage the fierce and fearsome feelings of desire, longing, and grief that bubble up in me, wanting to look at him but being terrified of what will happen if I do, and chastising myself when I don't. Knowing that the deeper into my experience I go, the harder it will be to leave them, and him, behind.

"I tell myself I can't keep doing this, and then reflexively begin calculating the number of days and hours I have to endure until I *do* do this . . . all over again."

I put down my notes and forced myself to look up at her. As soon as I caught her eyes, mine started to well up again. I was terrified she would tell me I was a freak of nature and needed to be sent to a research lab for further testing, and terrified she would tell me to stop seeing him.

Instead she replied, "That certainly sounds quite painful," her eyes squinting with warmth. "I really hear your dilemma. You are trying so hard to take care of him, and now you are, quite properly, asking how you can take care of yourself. Is this suffering worthwhile? It's a really good question, Cheryl."

Hearing this, I exhaled deeply.

After I filled her in a bit on what prompted me to start therapy with David—my mother's death, my helplessness in trying to heal my father, and my inability to feel safe with Alan—she practically chuckled when she said, "Well, Cheryl, given all of that, it's no wonder you have such strong feelings for David. It tells me you are doing good and important work. Good therapy is set up for this. The two of you have created a place where you feel safety and love, and that's a good thing. It's not your fault that you fell in love with him."

"Really? I asked, as if she were a priestess preparing to absolve me of my sins.

"Really."

"That said, it's important that what feels like an intense crush not become a crutch. I encourage you to use this as an opportunity to appreciate and experience all of your feelings—the love, the longing, the passion, and the anger—feelings that were perhaps denied to you as a child. David can take it."

Yes, but can I? I wondered to myself.

It was as if she were telling me to close my eyes while I was driving. Impossible. But, still desperate, I listened intently.

"Your time with David can be time spent coming back to yourself."

"Back to myself?" Myself was the last person I wanted to spend time with these days. I felt my stomach start to churn and glanced at the clock. I thought of asking her if she would mind if I gave her a small plant that would look nice next to her emerald-green lamp but decided against it.

Just as my tears were beginning to dry, she said something that started them flowing again.

"Cheryl, I feel fairly certain that if you left therapy now, it would be a mistake. Not only would you miss the chance to learn more about yourself and change your belief about why you can't have David, but you would also miss the chance to focus on and fight for your own needs and desires and move forward to get those needs met in other relationships."

I didn't realize it until she said it, that a part of me actually hoped she would order me to stop therapy with David immediately, or to come and do my work with her in her well-decorated, cozy-couched office. And even more achingly, I hoped that if I was miserable enough, she would save me from my longing for David. Just as I hoped that David would save me from my longing for my mother. Just as I hoped my mother would come back and save me from my longing for food. And just as I hoped my parents would save me from my longing for home when I was at camp.

Clearly, my time was up.

DARK CHOCOLATE

AND TRUE CRIME

Two weeks after my frenzied household purging of no-longer-needed stuff, I coerced my kids to join my campaign and had them sort through the books cramming their bedroom shelves. I figured it was easier for them to part with books than with treasured T-shirts and stuffed animals. My plan was to donate the books to our local library.

Becca and Andrew decided to make some fun of the drudgery and compete to see who could end up with the heaviest box in the smallest amount of time, without the box breaking. Becca narrowly won the competition, so Andrew had to carry both boxes into the kitchen. He offered to load them into my car, but I wanted to sort through the boxes first to make sure that in their competitive haste they hadn't parted with a book they might someday value once again.

The only book from Andrew's box that needed rescue was a copy of *The Jungle Book* inscribed by his maternal grandfather. I gently set it aside, imagining the day when Andrew might read it to one of his own children and share a treasured story about his granddaddy.

Three books into my inventory of Becca's castaways, my heart nearly skipped a beat. There it was—a hardback, dog-eared copy of *Gift from the Sea*, by Anne Morrow Lindbergh. It was my mom's favorite book, and this was a copy she had given me when I graduated from college. I must have placed it on Becca's bookshelf the night I read passages from it to her when she couldn't sleep. She had run out of interest in fairy tales.

I took a sip of the chamomile tea I had been drinking and moved onto the couch in our family room. My hands began to quiver as I opened the book, not quite knowing how it would read now that Mom was gone.

It was not surprising that her favorite book was *Gift from the Sea*. She loved the sea. When she was growing up in South Africa, being near it, playing in it, and taking comfort from its rhythms came naturally to her. I waded through the pages, read a few of the passages, and was struck by the surfeit of ways in which Mom took Ms. Lindbergh's insights to heart, inhabited them, and made them her own.

The most exhausting thing in life, I have discovered, is being insincere.

Mom could have written that line. She certainly lived it. She was unapologetically and consistently herself. No veneers. No pretense or preening. Her sole vanity was keeping her fingers and toes polished Candy Apple Red. Her manicurist of twenty-five years, Elisa, claimed Mom as her other mother and willingly commuted an hour each way to polish Mom's nails when she became too sick to drive.

When her hair turned prematurely gray—in fact, I don't remember her hair being anything other than shiny, wavy, and silver—she never considered dying it and chuckled when women stopped her in the grocery store or theater to ask for the name of her colorist.

Mom's sincerity also came through in her frankness. She was a blurter, often saying what came to her mind, or from her heart, without censure. Depending on the context, this could be refreshingly helpful ("Dear, you have some spinach in your teeth"), disarming ("So, Alan, what exactly went wrong in your first marriage?"), or downright embarrassing (as when she would announce to our waiter she was in the midst of a hot flash, and could he come back with a large glass of ice—no water?).

Good communication is as stimulating as black coffee and just as hard to sleep after.

Along with Mom's candor came an extrovert's gift for gab. Combined with her abundant curiosity and kindness for others, she made whomever she was with feel exquisitely interesting and worthwhile. She was on a first-name basis with nearly all of the merchants in her community—often enticing the butcher and dry cleaner to confess their life struggles within the space of a four-minute transaction. Saying, "Good morning. How are you?" wasn't a greeting to Mom—it was an invitation. She really wanted to know the answer. If she told you how beautiful you looked, you believed her.

I believe that true identity is found . . . in creative activity springing from within. It is found, paradoxically, when one loses oneself. A woman can best find herself in some kind of creative activity of her own.

Mom came to find her core identity, her strength, her sense of purpose and potency, though her work and her devotion to the synagogue she cofounded. She, along with my father and a few other Jewish families, saw a need in our community for a Reform Jewish synagogue and proceeded to help create one. And during the thirty-eight years she worked there, she served in just about every capacity except rabbi. She was the president of the congregation, chaired multiple committees, and became the office administrator and rabbi's assistant.

Mom told me once that if times had been different and she had gone to college, she would have studied psychology or criminology. Though she was a pacifist, an advocate for human rights, and a seeker of justice, I still found it startling that her favorite book genre was true crime. Perhaps it was her upbeat, pragmatic disposition, along with her deep curiosity about people, that allowed her to tolerate such grim reading.

And if criminology didn't work out, she could certainly have found success as an interior decorator—masterfully creating spaces that were both functional and beautiful. I was in awe of her unstudied confidence when choosing colors, arranging the furniture just so, or accessorizing a room.

One cannot collect all the beautiful shells on the beach. One can only collect a few. One moon shell is more impressive than three. There is only one moon in the sky.

Mom knew she could not collect all the beautiful shells on the beach, so she savored the ones she did gather. In fact, her ability to savor the little things in life was fundamental to her contentment. She cherished dark chocolate, extracrispy fries, hugs, her grandchildren, good books, deep conversations with friends, Phillies games, beauty anywhere and everywhere she found it, and, most of all, her time with Dad—her moon in the sky. Even during the worst days of her illness, she would smile and say to me, "This is the best time in my life. I have all the people I love around me."

The sea does not reward those who are too anxious, too greedy, or too impatient . . . Patience, patience, patience, is what the sea teaches.

This is perhaps the only one of Ms. Lindbergh's tenets that Mom did not embody. She was self-admittedly impatient and would even laugh as she confessed her impatience with being impatient, though she also acknowledged growing less so as she got older and adopted the mantra "It is what it is" to help keep her calm. Her sister liked to call her feisty, but I just saw her as eager.

Perhaps this is the most important thing for me to take back from beach living: simply the memory that each cycle of the tide is valid; each cycle of the wave is valid; each cycle of a relationship is valid.

Even as she planned diligently for the future, Mom absorbed and participated in the present moment better than anyone I have ever known, except perhaps my dog, Gracie. She was a realistic optimist with grand respect for and acceptance of the ebb and flow of life. She also appreciated, more than most, the seasonal cycles of life. Though she loved summertime, as it reminded her of home, fall became her favorite season, as she treasured the Jewish High Holidays, adored the inclusiveness of Thanksgiving, and marveled at the beauty of the leaves—often reminding me that she wept the first time she experienced autumn in the United States. Mom viewed the world with childlike wonder—greeting each day and experience as if it were the first time . . . and as if it were the last time. It was easy to astonish her.

Don't wish me happiness. I don't expect to be happy all the time. . . . It's gotten beyond that somehow. Wish me courage and strength and a sense of humor. I will need them all.

And indeed Mom would need them all—she needed them when, at nineteen years of age, she came to America for the first time—an immigrant and deeply homesick. She needed them when, six months later, she married a man who was also a homesick immigrant (though homesick for a home he'd never had.) And Mom certainly relied on these qualities when she became sick. In fact, instead of preaching the keys to a happy life, she lived them consistently and effortlessly, and, while they didn't give her a long life, they certainly made for a fulfilling one and, when it mattered most, a peaceful death.

As I read these passages, I could hear my mom's lyrical South African–accented voice speaking them. Waves of salty tears poured unbidden from my eyes. But this time, for the first time since she had died, the tears had as much relief in them as grief. *Maybe it's true*, I thought; *maybe she is still here—here in these words, here in the memories of how she lived them, and here in me. Maybe.*

INTO THE WOODS

I hoped the reassurances from the kindly female psychologist that my longings for David were both normal and valuable would diminish them—make them quietly fade away. I was wrong. I had a serious case of what I called "therapeutic chicken pox," a condition so distractingly itchy I agonized over when it would end and what scars would be left when it did.

A few months after our ten-week contract had expired and been renewed, I confessed, to my best friend, Jane, my pent-up desire to run into the woods with David and make love for three days. I was convinced that doing so would be more healing than talking. After she stopped laughing, she asked why I didn't fantasize about the Ritz-Carlton. But making love atop a soft bed of leaves, sheltered under a canopy of pines, spoke to the primitive and untamed nature of my longing.

At my next therapy appointment, I told David my pine-forested fantasy. And with great equanimity he said, "I think your desire is a statement of the aliveness that wants to be born in you."

Hmmm.

Before I could respond, he asked one of the questions I dreaded most: "Does this remind you of anything?"

I paused, rolled my eyes, and asked if the picture on the wall was new. It wasn't. Then I glanced at his clock and looked at my watch—convinced the clock was slow and our time should be up. It wasn't.

David asked again, "Cheryl, does the longing you are feeling so strongly for me remind you of anything?"

I sheepishly confessed, "Okay, so I did spend a great deal of time as a child, and a teenager, and a young woman, imagining the day I would fall into the welcoming embrace of a man who longed for me as much as I longed for him. And it would be wonderful. And it would be healing. And it would feel gobs better than this."

Damn. I was busted.

DISCONNECTED

I miss our phone calls most of all. Or, more specifically, the shared closeness I felt when talking with her on the phone. We spoke twice a week. I would call her on Wednesday mornings, and she would call me on Saturday mornings. I realize now how integral those calls were—not just as a way for me to connect with her, but as a way for me to connect with me.

When something good happens—one of my essays gets published, Alan lands a new deal, Gracie does something impossibly cute—I reflexively reach for the phone to tell Mom. When something not-so-good happens—one of my essays gets rejected, Alan and I have a fight, my cat pees on the carpet—I go to the phone, then stop short.

My phone-call confessionals with Mom began my junior year in college. I remember the watershed call that shifted the intimacy in our relationship from one of superficial questions and answers ("How are you?" "Fine." "What's been going on?" "Not much.") to something more authentic, deeper, truer.

It was the call when I revealed my relationship with Peter, the college administrator. Peter and I had just had our first fight—

something to do with his not being ready to introduce me to his friends. I wasn't planning on telling my mother about Peter or the fight, as I didn't want her to cast judgment or, worse, worry. But it was Tuesday at 7:00 PM, my designated weekly time to call home, and I didn't want to concern her by not calling, so I dutifully waited in line for the dormitory pay phone, angst and all.

As soon as Mom picked up the phone, she also picked up on the distress in my voice and asked what was wrong. In my vulnerability, I told her what was wrong and much more. I told her about Peter, how we had just argued about his reluctance to introduce me to his friends because I was a student, how great he was at his job, how he took me to real restaurants (not just the pizza-by-the-slice places my friends' boyfriends took them to), and how he owned his own condo one mile from the beach. And I even confessed that I was in love for the first time. And instead of freaking out about our age difference or questioning me about his intentions, she just listened. I was so relieved that I just kept talking. And then I began crying. At one point my roommate, Stacey, saw me sniffling on the phone and gently passed me a tissue.

While on the phone, I couldn't help thinking that I was crying not just because of my fight with Peter, but for all the times I had wanted to talk to my mom but hadn't been able to. I had just never believed she could handle what I was saying. I feared her need for me would prevent her from giving me the mothering I needed—prevent her from really hearing me. And I feared on some level I would risk disappointing her or, more likely, be left having to reassure her I was okay, as was historically the case. After all, I was her Poppet. And from my earliest days, she clung to me in ways that often felt more smothering than mothering. I remembered her telling me how scared she was of dropping me, breaking me, letting me out of her sight, and how important it was for her to braid my hair and adorn me in colorful floral dresses, although I much preferred being in solid-colored jumpers and wearing my hair down so it covered my eyes.

So there I was, sitting on the floor in the hallway of Laurel Hall, crying to my mom like the child I never felt safe enough to be. I don't remember resolving anything on the call, but I do remember hanging up with a sense of relief and acceptance unlike anything I had experienced between us before. This time she listened with interest, rather than judgment. This time I felt her compassion for me, rather than overwhelming concern. This time I could breathe.

After that "big reveal," our conversations started to flourish. I began seeking her opinions and sharing more of my interior life with her—good stuff about grades and friends, and the hard stuff, too. And she continued to listen and ask good questions— not the kind of questions that had an answer built into them, like, "You wouldn't really do that would, you?" but questions that helped me discover more about myself, like "Why is his opinion so important to you?" or "How does it feel to have a boyfriend who keeps you from his friends? What does that mean for you?" She also offered advice that felt wise and protective in a good way, like how I should stand up for myself with Peter and not let him take me for granted. I wonder now if it was advice she wished she had taken herself years before.

After college, I moved back near my parents to attend graduate school and then to live in my own apartment and begin my career. And while we still talked on the phone, because of our proximity we were also able to enjoy each other in person. We did typical mother-daughter things, like shop for clothes, decorate my succession of apartments ("Don't hang that picture too high"), and meet for lunch. Our relationship blossomed. And part of that blossoming included Mom's seeking my opinions. I felt quite adult when she asked for ideas on how to motivate synagogue volunteers, how to handle the rabbi, and what to say to Dad when he made comments about her weight and moped around the house, visibly depressed. She often said, with tears in her eyes, how much she valued my point of view and treasured the friendship we had. She knew many other mothers who wished they had this kind of relationship with their daughters, and she felt especially fortunate, as did I.

During those years, there were two topics that consistently summoned Mom's unsolicited advice. The first was my hair. Sometimes I would silently guess how many minutes it would take her to comment on it. Was I wearing it too curly, too long, too straight—or, worst, was it covering my eyes? Not only that, she would often remind me, and anyone within earshot, of the lengths she went to when I was a baby to get the swatch of red hair that stuck straight up on my head to lie down naturally.

Mom also made her opinion known when she thought I wasn't being my best self. Whether it was in a job or in a relationship, she didn't refrain from telling me, sometimes quite bluntly, when I was settling, missing something important, or just plain messing up. I complained to her once about a job that had turned quite toxic, and, after listening to me prattle on about my nutty colleagues, she said, "Cheryl, your colleagues may be nutty, but you are even nuttier for putting up with it. Stop kvetching and start looking for something else. You can do it."

I never admitted it, but I loved that she didn't always take my side. She was on the side of what was in my best interest, not what I wanted to hear.

Perhaps it was because I knew she would offer her truthful opinions that I held back from discussing some things with her. For instance, I didn't tell her about the darker aspects of my dating life, my loneliness, or many of the insights I was gleaning from therapy—especially about childhood. I felt ashamed of my pain, wanted to protect her from it, and didn't want her to feel responsible in any way.

After I married Alan, whom my mother adored, she maintained a respectful distance—never stopping by unannounced, and never assuming I'd be as available as I had been before I married. Yet we continued our ritual Wednesday and Saturday phone calls—the female equivalent of a father-and-son game of backyard catch. Back and forth. Easy. Grounding. For months after she died, I would find myself waiting for her call on Saturday mornings or reaching for the phone to call her on a Wednesday. And then, of course, I would remember.

Even though I managed my life effectively and considered myself quite independent, as did others, I had unknowingly become quite *dependent* on our phone conversations. So much so that if something happened and I couldn't tell her about it, I began to wonder if it had really occurred. Our talks allowed me to digest my life. The daily happenings, some positive, some not so positive, went down so much more easily with her there, on the other end of the line, to share them with.

I think that is in part why I feel so empty without her. I no longer have a way to gain perspective or even register my life as it unfolds. Without our phone calls, my life is a run-on sentence in search of a period. Our calls were that period for me. Which was lovely. And horrible. And part of the reason I feel so lost without her.

MY SAVING GRACIE

I t is 7:30 AM, and Gracie and I leave the house for our morning walk. We run down the hill at the foot of our street, slow down when we reach the art school parking lot, and come to a complete sit-stay before crossing the two-lane street running between the school and the park.

As soon as we step into the park, Gracie morphs into a full-nosed reconnaissance and begins her sniff-stroll-sniff-stroll saunter, smelling the crisp fallen leaves and tree trunks as if each has a secret to tell only her. Her nose is as probing and potent as the gadgets old men use to troll beaches in search of buried treasure, and it doesn't take long for her to find just the right oak at which to deposit the first of what seems like an endless supply of "pee-mail." A trickle here, a trickle there, each trickle a signature in an invisible doggie guest book: *Gracie was here.*

And thank God for that.

These walks, and this dog, have become my refuge. In fact, I often hum the song "You and Me Against the World," by Helen Reddy, while on our walks in honor of our solidarity. We welcomed Gracie into our family three weeks before I learned Mom was sick. She was a four- pound, creamy white, twelve-week-old Havanese with a caramel-colored stripe running along her spine, and seemingly bottomless, chocolate Tootsie Pop–colored eyes. Friends warned me that having a puppy was like having a baby who never grows up. But I acquiesced after Becca pleadingly assured Alan and me that a dog would cure the insomnia that had plagued her since Andrew had left for boarding school. I dearly wanted Becca, and by extension me, to sleep through the night, and certainly understood her longing for companionship. In addition, this was probably my last chance to bring a baby of any breed into my life, and I wanted to grab it. Still, even I could not have predicted how off-the-cliff in love I would fall for Gracie, how much of my own loneliness she would assuage, and how essential her puppy presence would become to me.

Puppy training classes had been a welcome distraction from the frenzied world of Mom's cancer treatment that had suffused my days, and often provided a unique juxtaposition between caring for Gracie and caring for my mom. During one evening class, just as Gracie and I were practicing the sit-stay command, I received an exasperated phone call from Mom. She had been pressing her call button for over an hour, and no nurse had come to her room to help her out of bed. The irony that I couldn't will Gracie to sit and I couldn't will my mother to stand was not wasted on me. Nor was the deeper truth that, despite my best efforts, I was powerless to cajole either of them to heal.

But oh, how I tried. I even took Gracie to the nursing home a few times to offer Mom some unwieldy pet therapy. Gracie bounced through the hallways and stormed into Mom's room like a manic bunny rabbit, settling down only when I placed her on Mom's bed to smother her face with kisses. Then, exhausted from the ruckus, both of them promptly fell asleep. Seeing Gracie and Mom lying peacefully together provided me with a respite from the otherwise wrenching guilt and separation anxiety I felt every time I left one of them to tend to the other.

Back on our walk, Gracie's floppy angel-wing ears rise when she spots her four-footed friend Dora the Dalmation. She speeds toward her friend as if she is now walking me (which, of course, she is.) I laugh to myself when I think how little of what we were taught in puppy school has made its way into the park.

Gracie and I cross the wooden bridge that spans a narrow stream. Then the path winds past a placid duck pond. Upon seeing the ducks and geese, Gracie puts on her best bully imitation and begins barking and fake-lunging at them—just for the pleasure of seeing them scatter.

When we return home, I take off Gracie's harness and she jumps on my leg to greet me as if she hasn't seen me all morning. Then she bounds into a short version of her happy dance, which involves running in circles with her favorite stuffed groundhog, Porky, while squealing and snorting in equal measure. If this were the longer version of the happy dance and I were actually returning home after having been out for a few hours, I would excitedly call, "Gracie," open my arms wide, and fall face-first on the rug, my hair covering my face. At which point Gracie would drop Porky and begin determinedly digging through my hair in search of my face, using her own face as a probe. And when I start laughing (something I do more readily with her than with any other being), she takes full advantage and gives me a big lick on my lips. I try not to think about where her tongue has been that day or about the story on the evening news on the perils of being kissed by one's dog, and instead surrender to the love.

Gracie laps up some water and settles into the plaid dog bed next to my desk, and, as often happens after we experience a playful, tender interlude, I recall that not every moment with her has been so carefree. I flash to the night when, still in the midst of house-breaking her, I reached into her pen to take her outside for her final potty of the day. She had been sleeping, and as I approached, she growled at me. Unwisely, I continued my approach and picked her up, only to have her growl again and then bite me. Hard. On my wrist. I knew she had done it on purpose, because she bit me a second time. And I cried. Not because she broke my skin, but because she broke my heart. It was like the first fight with a new boyfriend. *Not you, too,* I thought. *Not my perfect puppy. How could you?*

Too shocked to even yell at her, I called the dog trainer, who, before telling me how to proceed, reminded me that a badly behaved dog is always accompanied by a badly behaved owner. So of course I spent the rest of the night in the proverbial doghouse, blaming myself for what happened. And despite the fact that I made up with Gracie the next morning (I'm a sucker for her "flop and drop"—when she falls on her back and presents her pink, tender tummy for me to kiss), I couldn't shake the truth that at some point, everyone bites. Life hurts.

What made my closeness with Gracie all the more vital was the distance between Alan and me at the time. Alan didn't know how to befriend me in my grief, and I didn't know how to ask for the consolation I desperately wanted. Plus, I found myself mired in resentment when he refused to help care for Gracie and referred to her as "it" most of the first year. David was spot-on when he offered that the way I felt with Gracie was how I felt with Alan during our courtship—safe, playful, affectionate. Perhaps Alan sensed this and was acting out of jealousy—the same way first-time fathers often do.

When my heart hurts, as it does most of the time these days, Gracie, now curled up and sleeping soundly, is a most capable bereavement counselor. In her company I feel safe enough to weep without worrying about burdening an actual human being. When I share my woes and dilemmas with her, anything from "Gracie, I feel like the only daughter in the history of the universe who has ever lost a mother she loved and needed" to "Gracie, should I make pork chops or pasta for dinner tonight?" she cocks her sweet, doe-eyed face to the right, squints like she is trying to read a fortune cookie without her glasses, and gazes up at me, as if to ask, *Why so sad?* Then I cup my hands around her face, kiss the bridge of her nose, and respond, "Thank you, Gracie. Thank you for trying so hard to understand me."

Gracie is more than my grief counselor, more than my most abiding companion, my pseudochild, my secret-keeper extraordinaire. She is my role model. She exemplifies so many of the qualities I struggle with: She lives fully in the present moment, her thoughts never wandering to past regrets or future potentialities. She unabashedly expresses her feelings, even the difficult ones. She is goofy just for the sake of being goofy. She naps without guilt and has no trouble claiming her hungers for food, play, and affection—though snatching the first *and* last piece of cake is something we are still working on.

I've read that people grow to look like their dogs. I certainly wouldn't mind that—Gracie's wavy hair is to die for! But what I aspire to even more is becoming more like her on the inside, unleashing the Gracie-ness in me: claiming my hungers even if they can't always be satisfied; playing with people, not just pets, with abandon; savoring the present; and believing I am worthy and deserving of what I want—even if what I want is the last piece of cake.

LETTER TO MY UNBORN CHILD

It's Mother's Day. While I am not surprised that my grief for Mom is more acute today, I am surprised by the eruption of longing I feel for you.

Part of me hoped spending the day with you would absorb the homesickness I feel for her—that I could comfort myself knowing a part of Mom, and someday a part of me, would live on through you. But instead of finding comfort or even distraction from my pain, my motherless and childless status leaves me feeling doubly bereft, like a book without bookends.

Suddenly I'm awash with questions. How could I—a woman with such deeply maternal tendencies that I happily nurture a menagerie of pets, fistfuls of friends and family, a house, and houseplants—not have had a child of my own?

How did this happen? How did I not do this most natural, obvious thing—and, more important, why? What does not bearing you say about me? Am I a failure for not embracing the most important (some would say noble) role of a woman's life? Am I somehow a less attractive woman? Did I disappoint my mom by not giving her another grandchild?

Like most girls, I expected to one day be a wife and mother. I even played the "what would I name my children?" game with friends—Scott if you were a boy, and Skye if you were a girl. So I know I thought of you, wanted you, and dreamed of you.

My opportunity to actually have you was delayed when, during my twenties and thirties, I dated a succession of charmingly unavailable men. I was holding out for a fantastical Mr. Right, yet masking my own unavailability by choosing Mr. Wrong. As my impatience grew, I considered becoming a single parent a few times, but my commitment to my someday soul mate was so strong, I was afraid if I stopped looking for him and had you on my own, he would never arrive.

I even entered therapy to clear any psychic cobwebs keeping me from finding Mr. Right. And to a large extent, it worked. I uncovered and replaced the belief that I had nothing to offer with the more accurate possibility that I had buckets of love to give and there had to be, just had to be, a man out there in need of that love, and together our love would give birth to you.

Shortly thereafter I met Alan, a divorcing dad who, along with his two beautiful children, Andrew and Becca, was indeed in need of some love and healing. Partly because his kids were young enough and welcoming enough for me to actively participate in their upbringing, my desire for you subsided as I put my energy into building a new home and family.

So, for a long time, this story of why I didn't give birth to you made perfect sense. I just ran out of time, and then ran out of need once I became a stepmom. But in the wake of Mom's death, my story has started to unravel and I am questioning more deeply why I haven't scrambled to bring you into this world.

The unraveling first emerged in the form of fear. I selfishly wondered, Who will tend to me, keep my toes warm, and make sure I get my pain medicine on time when I am too old or sick to do it myself? (Even though I know, rationally, having biological children provides no guarantee of such care.)

And it continues as I acknowledge that as loving and accepting as Andrew and Becca are, I will never be their first call when they are sick or overjoyed and never the one they send their Mother's Day cards to.

I've also been feeling stronger pangs of longing when I see new moms with their babies at the playground while walking Gracie, and at less expected times, like when I'm filling out a form asking if I have children, or when strangers comment to Becca and me how much we look alike—assuming we are mother and daughter.

Baby, please know that the reason I did not give you life is not because I would not love you. It is because of my penetrating and paralyzing fear of what a love that strong would do to me, and what I might do to you in the name of that love. And I couldn't bear it. So I bear the regret instead.

You see, for a long time, I truly believed the most loving thing I could do for you was not to have you. That, as weird and paradoxical as that sounds, I saved you from me.

In fact, have I mentioned that I'm no good at fun? I don't know how to play. Never did. And I'm lousy at sewing costumes, making fudge, and keeping score at baseball games. I quickly get bored playing board games, and don't get me started on my impatience with silly and scary movies. And, despite ten years of summer camp, I don't get along well with little kids. The fact is, I never experienced my childhood as a child, so how can I shepherd you through yours?

You see, I've learned a thing or two about what a child needs and the pain and cost of not getting those needs met. I would be forever trying to give you what I didn't have and maybe still don't have. And I am so afraid that I would fail you, and that, despite my best efforts, I wouldn't be enough to spare you pain. And I'm not sure I could survive that.

I know this might sound strange to you, but in many ways, I already have a baby—my dog, Gracie. I told Alan he should imagine she came straight from my loins. But even so, look how I mess things up with her—I project my separation anxiety onto her, let the groomer pin frilly pink bows to her ears, and sometimes indulge her with two dog treats at dinner instead of one, when no one is looking.

And you would be the real fruit of my loins, which means in addition to all that, you would risk inheriting my propensity for self-loathing, codependence, chubby thighs, and unruly hair. See all that I saved you from?

Just last week I saw a headline about a famous female movie star about my age adopting a baby, and I thought for a moment, Yes, I can do that. I'm not too old to adopt and doing so would spare you my emotional and biological in-

heritance, but it wouldn't spare me the fear that I would still find a way to mess up.

And, just as true, when I look into my heart and consider my life as it is right now, I know that while I do want to give birth to something, it's no longer a child. That time has passed.

And so I grieve—as much for the me who never felt worthy of you as for you. For what I now know is that as much as I prevented hurting you by not bringing you into the world, I also hurt myself by not allowing myself to receive the love and joy you would undoubtedly have brought me. It's a trade-off I'm not sure I would make if I had my life to live over again.

David asked me, just a few weeks ago, if I was glad I was born, even though I had a painful childhood. I answered yes. I'm glad I was born.

And maybe, if I had had you, hurts and all, you would have one day answered the same. I'm so sorry neither of us will ever know.

Love,
Mommy

WWMD? (WHAT WOULD MOM DO?)

One afternoon nine months after Mom died, my sister-in-law, Jamie, called me from her home in Georgia. Something in her soft, Southern "Hi there, sis" seemed askew.

"I'm sorry to put y'all through this so soon after we lost your mom, and there's no good way to say it, so I'll just spit it out. I have breast cancer. It's stage three. I'm having both breasts and some lymph nodes removed later this month."

It took me a painstakingly long moment to comprehend her news. I actually stood up and shook my head the way Gracie shakes hers when she's startled or confused. My pause lasted so long, Jamie asked if I was still on the line and had heard what she said.

Yes, I was still on the line. But no, I couldn't have heard her correctly. She was just forty-six years old. Her mother had died prematurely from the same cancer, so Jamie had been vigilant about getting regular checkups. She was one of the few women I knew who actually did breast self-exams in the shower each month. She exercised. She ate kale before kale was cool. She never ate meat or drank alcohol, except for a few sips of eggnog each

December. Not only that, Jamie was waist-deep in planning a bar mitzvah for her son, Ben. Cancer could not be happening. Not to her. Not now. Hadn't our family already paid our cancer dues?

And stage III, no less. I was overcome with the same sinking feeling I'd had when the oncologist had told us Mom's cancer was already at stage IV when they found it. How could cancer be that sneaky? Where had we been when it was at stages I, II, and III? How could a person be walking around and not even know she had this time bomb inside her? I felt like the Rice women were under siege and selfishly wondered if I was next. Why shouldn't I be? If cancer could steal my otherwise healthy mom in six months, and if it could sneak up on Jamie despite all she had done to prevent it, then surely it was only a matter of moments before it blindsided me. Maybe it already had. I made a mental note to schedule the mammogram I'd been postponing.

Jamie told me that an ominous dream was what had prompted a visit to her gynecologist in between checkups. *More like a nightmare*, I wanted to say but didn't. She was pushing to have the operation as soon as possible and was expecting to hear back from the surgeon about his availability within the next day or so. She didn't want to wait until after the bar mitzvah. Cancer was not on the guest list.

After we ended our call, I instinctively wanted to phone Mom—my ever-dependable crisis counselor. She always provided just the right words to calm me down and keep me from catastrophizing. But since a phone conversation was not an option, I curled myself up in the window seat in my home office, closed my eyes, and imagined what she'd say if I was able to talk to her. She, too, would be shocked and concerned, but since helplessness was not part of her repertoire, she'd also provide some good ideas on what to do next.

Cheryl, it will be fine, I could hear her saying. *Let's not get ahead of ourselves. The good news is, they found the cancer and can do something about it. Jamie is young and strong. She will beat this. No doubt about it. Now, I want you to jump on the Internet and compare airfares and flight schedules to Atlanta. You must be prepared to book your flight immediately once you know the date of her surgery. And have Alan send Mark that book he gave Dad about how to care for a wife who is going through cancer. He'll read it if it comes from Alan.*

"Good advice, Mom." I whispered.

I immediately went to my computer to do as she said. *Okay,* I thought. *Maybe I can do this.*

⁂

While I felt wretched on Jamie's behalf, I was also deeply concerned for Mark. How would he handle this just a few months after losing Mom? Mark was eighteen months younger than I was, and I had always felt protective of him. I committed my only act of physical violence on his behalf when we were in grade school. Our neighborhood bully, Quinton, picked a fight with Mark during a kickball game. Quinton was as brawny as Mark was scrawny. He didn't pummel Mark with punches; he just tripped him as he was running to first base and then sat on him.

I was horrified. I thought Mark was being suffocated and ran full speed from third base to the scene of the crime, screaming at the top of my little lungs, "Get off my brother, you beast!" before hitting Quinton in his fleshy arm. My guess is, the only reason my heroics worked and Quinton stood up was that he and all of the neighborhood kids who had formed a circle around us were so shocked at my show of unbridled might that they lost all focus on the purpose and pleasure of a good fight. Mark, however, felt humiliated and was angrier at me for rescuing him than he was at Quinton for squashing him. Still, I would do it again in a heartbeat.

While Mark was no longer a scrawny boy, I was still a protective big sister who was chronically committed to making sure the men in her life didn't suffer. But now I wasn't quite sure what I would do for him. He often kept his feelings hidden and had inherited Mom's fierce focus on the positive side of life. I was in awe when I called to see how he was doing on Mother's Day and found him functioning much better than I was. He said he was choosing to be grateful that he had had such a wonderful mom, and found solace in his commitment to keeping her alive by remembering her every day. I wasn't sure if he was in denial or had achieved a level of equanimity I could only dream of.

Without invitation, I heard Mom's voice again: *You don't have to* do *anything for him, Cheryl. Just be there.*

The next day, I called Mark and learned that Jamie's surgery was scheduled for the following Wednesday. I told him that unless he felt I would be in the way, I would come down the day before the surgery and stay with them until Jamie was settled back home. The thought of Mark being alone in a waiting room was impossible for me to bear. I wanted to be there for him and the kids as much as for Jamie. The relief in his voice when he heard my plans was palpable.

I spent the night before my trip drenched in worry. I was worried about leaving Gracie in Alan's sole care for the first time (hence my four-page list of instructions, including the phone numbers of the veterinarian and friends to call if Alan felt over-matched); worried about saying and doing the right things for Jamie, Mark, Ben, and Ben's sister, Rachel; and, most of all, worried about doing it all without Mom's wisdom to guide me. Mom should be going instead of me. I felt like a fraud—like the second-string quarterback coming into the game because the superstar starter has been permanently sidelined.

As I packed my suitcase, I went to my dresser and took out the black velvet–covered box holding Mom's opal engagement ring. She had given it to me, along with her wedding band, on her first emergency hospital visit during her cancer treatment. The rings had no longer fit her, as her fingers had become swollen from the steroids she was taking. At first I'd felt awkward even holding them, but she had assured me that she felt better knowing they would be in my care, and had added offhandedly, "You're going to end up with them anyway."

For the first time, I put the opal on my right-hand ring finger. It felt strange seeing the ring I had admired on Mom's hand for decades now on mine. Mom wore little jewelry except for these rings, and they looked radiant on her. Her hands were beautiful, accentuated by her signature red nail polish. I scolded myself for the poor condition my own nails were in and vowed to take better care of them—especially if I was to continue wearing her ring.

I pulled out my carry-on bag and added my writing journal, a pack of Twizzlers for an emergency sugar fix, and a book of Mary Oliver poems. I was as ready as I could be.

To settle myself on the plane ride, I wrote down my intentions for the trip: *Be tuned in. Be present. Be helpful. Be patient.* David had encouraged me to periodically check in with myself about how I was feeling, so I added, *Right now, I am feeling scared. And bereft. And a little bit queasy.*

Hours later, when I walked into Jamie and Mark's home, I was taken aback by how calm and strong Jamie looked. She had a freshly cut, honey-colored bob. She was dressed in her signature purple paisley collared shirt, Gap jeans, and running shoes. Her aqua-blue eyes were as big and sparkly as ever. Mark often said that his first look into her eyes was his last look at any other woman.

But beyond her outer beauty, it was her strength of character, can-do attitude, and penchant for action that I admired. I hardly ever saw her sitting down, unless it was to sew a costume or read a book to one of the kids. I often joked that Jamie would have thrived as a pioneer woman out on the prairie, and that if we had lived during those times, I would have fought to take up residence on her homestead. She was fit, resourceful, and determined. She was also a fiercely devoted mother with a lot of life in her and a lot of life yet to live. I trusted these qualities would serve her well now. I suddenly felt flooded by how much she and my mom were alike.

After I unpacked my bag, Mark and I drove the route to and from their house and the hospital and reviewed the schedule for the following day.

"How are you doing?" I asked.

"Fine. The doctor is one of the best. I know Jamie is in good hands."

"Well, that's good. It's important to have confidence in your doctor. I know that meant a lot to Mom." *Damn. Why did I say that? Mom died. Who cares what she thought about her doctor?* I attempt a quick recovery by trying to say the *right* thing this time.

"Is there anything I can do for *you*? I can't imagine how hard it is. I know you're still grieving Mom."

"No. You're already doing it. I know it's helping the kids to have you here."

I was amazed at how matter-of-fact he was being. Perhaps it was the newspaper reporter in him that allowed his default demeanor to be one of objectivity.

That night we all went out for an early Mexican dinner. I tried to think of how Mom would keep the conversation light and tried to follow her imagined lead by showering the kids with questions about school and friends. I thought I was doing well, but soon after, I made my biggest blunder yet. After dinner, when Jamie announced she was going to bed early, I sheepishly followed her to the bedroom.

"So, I know this might sound silly, but I was wondering if you perhaps wanted us to hold some sort of good-bye ceremony for your breasts. I googled a few options before I left, just in case."

As soon as I said it, I realized Mom would never have suggested something so New Agey to Jamie, or to anyone, for that matter. What was I thinking?

Jamie giggled for a moment but then looked down and said rather sullenly, "No, thanks. They feel poisoned, and I just want them gone."

"That makes sense." I muttered. "I'm sorry for being so ridiculous. I guess it was the life coach in me. Forgive me." I also wanted to apologize for not bringing Mom along, but I knew that would sound as silly as having a funeral for her breasts.

"Can I bring you some water?" I asked, going for the rebound.

"That would be great."

The next morning, the kids woke up and readied themselves for school without my having to do much besides wonder what they were thinking and if it was better to ask or just stay silent. Over our waffles, I assured the kids I'd be there to have dinner with them and told them what they already knew: their mom was strong, she loved them more than anything, and she would be okay. It wasn't lost on me how committed I had been, at her request, to telling Mom the truth about her condition as it unfolded, but since I had made no such promise to Ben and Rachel and none of us really knew the full truth of Jamie's condition, staying positive seemed best. I hoped Mom would understand.

Before Mom got sick, I hadn't been in a hospital in decades, and now here I was, back in one just nine months later. And other than the sweet Southern accents of most of the staff, the look, sound, and smell of both places were the same.

I caught up with Jamie and Mark just as they were being escorted from admissions to the pre-op station. I wasn't sure if Jamie wanted me to go in with her, so I stepped back. Then she turned to me and said, "Let's go, sis."

As I sat in a chair next to Jamie's gurney, I felt small, like I needed the wisdom and guidance of my mother—or of Jamie's mom, or my dad, or any parent—more than ever. Even when I had been taking care of Mom during her illness, and even when the cancer had muddled her brain and made her more child-like than parental, I still felt like a daughter taking care of her mother—the real grown-up was still there. But now, as I sat with Jamie and Mark, I realized *we were* the grown-ups. We had to take care of each other. Without warning, we had bumped up a generation and been promoted. I felt completely unprepared for this new role.

As if reading my mind, Jamie turned to me and said, "I miss your mom."

I stepped out of my chair and walked to the side of her bed, "Me, too. One time during Mom's illness, I walked into her room to find her weeping. When I asked what was wrong, she softly cried, 'I really wish my mom were here.' I guess no matter how old we are, there are always times we just want our mothers." I started to tear up. I felt so completely overmatched by this task: inadequate and inept. I wasn't Mom. I wasn't Jamie's mom. Truth be told, I wasn't anyone's mom.

Then, as if we had summoned them from beyond, the oddest string of coincidences began to occur. The pre-op nurse came in and introduced herself to us as Diane, the same name as Jamie's sister, who lived far away. This prompted Jamie to recall that the name of the woman from admissions who registered her that morning was Cheryl. And things got even spookier when the operating nurse came into our pre-op station and introduced herself as Wendy—my mom's name—at which point Jamie's tears began to flow as well. And later on, just to complete the party, the recovery-room nurse showed up with a name tag reading JILL—the same name as Jamie's mom. The saints had come marching in. Maybe we weren't as alone as I had imagined after all.

Mark was very tender toward and solicitous of Jamie. And I was struck by watching his newspaper reporter skills come to the fore as he peppered the nurses and doctors with questions that neither Jamie or I had thought to ask. Clearly, he was up for this.

After Jamie was sedated and wheeled into surgery, I hurried to get Mark and me some coffee and told him I'd catch up with him in the waiting room. I couldn't resist also buying another pack of Twizzlers and some gummy bears to give to Ben and Rachel later on.

I had been worried about leaving Mark alone, but, much to my astonishment, when I walked into the waiting room, I could hardly find a seat. My first thought was, *Wow—they must have booked a lot of surgeries today.* But then I saw Mark working the room as if he were hosting a cocktail party. When he saw me, he waved me over and began making introductions to the numerous members of his and Jamie's synagogue and to his colleagues. Everyone who greeted me gave me a hug. "We've heard so much about you." "So sorry to meet you under these circumstances." "Jamie and Mark are the heart and soul of our temple." "Anything we can do for them, you just let us know. Let me give you my phone number." One woman also gave me a three-page schedule listing menus and dates for meal delivery for the next two weeks!

Every time Mark and Jamie visited us in Philly, I chided them about living so far away from family and selfishly encouraged them to move up north. But now, seeing the throng of friends gathered, I couldn't help but think it was I who should be moving.

That afternoon, in her hospital room after her surgery, Jamie was understandably exhausted and weepy. A bit later, her doctor came in to check on her.

"So, the surgery went very well. We won't know for sure until we get the pathology back, but from what I can tell, I think we got out what we needed. Now tell me, darlin', how are you feeling? How's the pain?"

"Well, the pain's fine, but can you give me something to dam up these tear ducts? I'm weeping like a baby. This is ridiculous."

Mark, the doctor, and I let out a collective laugh.

"No, honey, I'm afraid I can't give you anything you don't need. And if your body needs to weep, then let it weep. I know if I'd just had major surgery, I'd be weeping, too."

It was reassuring to see that, breasts or no breasts, our Jamie was still here. And it seemed like she was in very good, caring hands.

That evening, back at their home, I tried to comfort Ben and Rachel over plates of spaghetti by telling them how brave and strong their mom had been that day, and how loving their dad was being. Hearing it from me was one thing, but they didn't truly seem to take a breath until they spoke with Jamie and Mark by phone a bit later on. And I tried not to take it personally when Rachel looked up at me and said I wasn't doing the voices right as I read her bedtime story to her.

Jamie was discharged from the hospital the next day. (The spell had been broken, as her discharge nurse's name was Claudia. We didn't know any Claudias.) I was fairly useless at helping to change Jamie's dressings but pretty good at keeping the kids engaged so she could rest. Thankfully, a good friend of Jamie's was a nurse and more than willing to help with the post-op care.

Since Jamie was not one to stay in bed and rest, I realized that the best gift I could give her was some semblance of normalcy, so the next day I said my good-byes and started my trip home.

I made it to the airport just in time to call David for our regularly scheduled session. I was grateful he agreed to do it by phone, as he knew I was particularly uptight about the trip. As usual, I was both eager and nervous to speak with him.

"I'm here at the airport. My plane doesn't board for another ninety minutes. Let me say up front that I did a very poor job of checking in with myself on what I was feeling at various times during the trip."

"Given all that was going on, it makes sense that that would be the case. As you look back on it now, what *were* some of your feelings during your visit?"

I told David how moving it was being with all of them—how inspiring Jamie's courage was, and how I couldn't imagine calling Mark my little brother ever again now that I had seen the husband, father, and community member he had become.

I noticed how much freer I felt talking with David on the phone than I did in person. It was such a relief not having to struggle to make eye contact.

"What was it like for you to see that—that you didn't need to rescue Mark?"

"It was a bit humbling, to tell you the truth, seeing him step up like that. I was worried they would be alone in this, but they have tons of friends who really care about them. And, just like Mom, they have found a home in their synagogue. It was quite inspiring."

"You mean, *you felt* inspired?"

"Yes. I felt inspired. In fact, I'm thinking that perhaps I'll explore ways of getting involved in our synagogue when I get home. As I was leaving, I told Mark that Mom would have been proud of both of them. It was the first time he cried."

"You mentioned before your trip that you were concerned about getting through this without your mom. How did that part go for you?"

"It was really, really hard being there without her. At first I felt like an impostor and kept asking myself what she would say or do to make things better. But eventually, that self-conscious-ness got in my way."

As we continued our call, another memory of my visit popped in my mind.

"I read a bedtime story to my niece, and I realized that, without intending to, I was using my mom's inflections. I mean, what do I know about reading to little kids?"

"And what happened?"

"And then suddenly a different voice came to me—an accented one, for sure, but it was *mine*."

"That's big, Cheryl. Really big. Do you think your mom would have been proud of you, too?"

I gulped back tears.

"Yes. I do."

A few hours later, I arrived home. Gracie was her tail-wagging, tongue-licking self, which didn't surprise me, as Alan had been texting me details of her every pee and poop since I'd left. When I stepped into the hot bath Alan had run for me, I thought about cancer and the slipperiness of life. How naive I had been to believe that bad things were over for us. I wondered what the future would hold for Jamie and Mark. The surgery was behind her, but her treatment was just beginning. Sinking deeper into the warm water, I lifted up my hand to once more admire Mom's ring. Tomorrow I would pick up some nail polish. Not Candy Apple Red—perhaps a soft mauve instead.

FINALLY, A FLURRY—OKAY,

AN AVALANCHE—OF ANGER

I guess it was inevitable. David put me over the edge. It began when I asked him when his birthday was. I asked him not because I wanted to see if our astrological signs were compatible (though it wasn't inconceivable for me to have Googled it), but because I wanted to celebrate him on his special day, if not with a cupcake or a funny card—which I knew, based on his no-gifts policy, he would refuse—then at least with a sincere "Happy birthday. I hope you have a healthy and joyful year." Was that too much to ask?

This wasn't the first time David had refused to answer a question about himself. Over the course of our sessions, I had inquired about his favorite movie, how he came to be a psychologist, and whether or not he had a dog. I had refrained from asking him more personal questions, like when the last time he had cried was, and why; how often he made love to his wife, and what they fought about; and what brought him joy. I just didn't have the guts.

"When is your birthday, David?"

"I'm not going to answer that, as it's not relevant to your work. But I am curious to know why you want to know, and how my not telling you makes you feel."

Again, was this too much to ask? For him to share a simple fact he would not hesitate to share with his dry cleaner, his next-door neighbor, or even a stranger on an airplane—anyone else in the whole wide world, it seemed, but me? I had reached my limit.

This time, I wasn't just frustrated; I was enraged. And when I came home from our session, I stomped directly to my computer and furiously typed this letter.

Dear David,

Fuck you!

You are not a professional psychologist. You are a professional tease with a PhD in voyeurism. You are not my friend, my family, my lover, or my healer. You are a psychological sadist who gets off on being the object of other people's deepest fantasies and idealizations while risking nothing of yourself.

You flawlessly lured me in, seducing me into lowering my guard, making me feel hungry and gushy to the point where the only thing that made sense was expressing my feelings for you. And then, BAM! You conveniently morphed into love's executioner by saying I'm not wrong for wanting you—just don't think there is a chance in hell of having you. I actually have a greater chance of winning the lottery than of winning you. But you will gladly sell me another ticket!

Fuck you AGAIN!

*I have gone to the hard places. I have revealed my ten-
der spots, told you my stories, despite how treacherous it has
felt. You know me from the inside out. I have been a great
patient, but clearly not a great enough person to even know
your birthday!*

*You want me to cry here—would that make you feel bet-
ter? Do you think it will make me feel better? It would make
me feel small, scared, ugly, and defeated.*

*You want me to tell you humiliating things—why? So
you can feel bigger and better in comparison?*

*You want me to look at you so you can see my pain?
Don't you know how ashamed I am of my wounds? How sure
I am my pain will kill you?*

*If you really want to help me, then talk to me! Tell me
what you long for, whom you long for. Then hold me close.
Close enough for me to hear your heart beating. Then fuck
me. Yes, me—the good girl—wants you to fuck her. Hard.
Then I'll cry. Then I'll scream. Then you'll be in this, too, and
maybe we'll both be healed. Yes—I think you need healing
from your sadism. Or not. But at least I won't be alone.*

*I am so mad at you. I can hardly remember why I
started therapy. Oh, right—to grieve. First my mom, then
my childhood, then my marriage, and now you. Oh, the joy.*

*Why can't you change the rules for once? How do you
know they are helping me? They feel like they are choking
the life out of me.*

*You tell me that you care for all of your patients—that
everyone falls in love with their therapist. Is that supposed to
make me feel better? It makes me feel like a fucking cliché.
Like an uninteresting, unoriginal, gullible, pathetic sucker.*

You tell me nothing about yourself, and yet you always encourage me to ask you questions, and when I do, I end up feeling humiliated—like a foolish bird who crashes beak-first into a glass window again and again.

You say it would be easier for you to tell me your stories, your birthday, your favorite movie, but that's not true. Withholding your preferences and perversities keeps you immune to rejection and maintains your rock star status—just like it did my dad. And like him, you have masterfully turned me into your number-one groupie.

I hate you for not loving me the way I want. You could heal me. I'm convinced of it. Talk to me like a friend. Kiss me like a lover. Why can't you imagine it being beautiful instead of hideous, passionate instead of painful? Why can't you just appreciate and enjoy what I have to give you, instead of continuing to shine the fluorescent light of suspicion onto my every motivation?

I am so lost. Why am I here? Is it to learn how to be free of attachments or to learn how to have them? Is it to learn how to be close and intimate or to accept that I am ultimately alone? This experience has pierced something so deep inside me—so many hungers. Why acknowledge them if they can't be fed?

I don't know right now if you are my ally or my enemy. I am terrified of staying in therapy and terrified of leaving. Is this healing or is it hell?

Right now it just feels like hell.

Sincerely,
Cheryl

My heart was pounding like a racehorse's when I read David the letter. It was the meanest and possibly truest letter I had ever written, let alone read out loud. I was sure he was going to fire me. Send me packing. Tell me our time was up—for good. But instead David looked at me with earnest eyes and said, "Well, Cheryl, it's about time you got angry. You are so brave."

GAME DAY

I was pleasantly surprised my dad agreed to continue our tradition of attending the Father's Day Phillies game together. For years he and Mom had split a two-seat, thirteen-game Sunday package with Alan and me. Typically, my parents went to six games, Alan and I went to six games, and Dad and I attended the Father's Day game.

My father had yet to attend a public event since Mom had died. He was still learning how to be in the world without her, as was I, and going to places he and Mom enjoyed together was especially difficult. So I took it as a positive sign that, despite his discomfort, he agreed to come. In fact, I even found myself quietly hoping that attending the game would begin to unite us in our grief, the way we had united in our care for Mom when she was dying. And even more, maybe, I thought, now that he was my sole remaining parent, he would step up to the plate and into my life with unprecedented zeal. Maybe he could finally be my *daddy*, my hero, and rescue me from the sea of grief I was bobbing in.

I had always looked up to my father, seen him as larger than life. His professional reputation as a highly successful advertising executive and beloved college professor made him renowned, not just in his field, but in the community as well. The fact that he often used his own voice in the radio and TV commercials he wrote and produced added to his celebrity. I was in awe of the media and teaching awards regularly bestowed on him and the pride I felt when reading the many heartfelt thank-you notes he received from students and protégés. The fact that he made such an impact on others while privately struggling with chronic physical and emotional ailments rendered him heroic in my eyes.

But any hopes about his fitness for being my hero now were dashed as soon as I climbed in his car. The stench of his sorrow was so thick, it literally took my breath away. I opened the passenger-side window, eager for it to escape.

"How are you doing, Dad?" I asked, even though the answer was palpable.

"Okay. I'm trying. I really am. You know there's no road map for this."

"I know, Dad. I can't imagine how hard it is for you. And it must be very difficult going to the ballpark without Mom. We don't have to go, you know. We can go for a walk instead."

"No. I want to go. I told Mom about it this morning. It means a lot to her that we are going."

In addition to struggling to find my own new relationship to Mom, I was also struggling to accept my father's efforts to do the same. As much as I tried, I hadn't quite gotten used to the idiosyncratic ways in which he was navigating the territory, which included relaying his graveside conversations with Mom as if she were still alive, and letting me know via email how he was preparing to reunite with her in death so she wouldn't have to be alone. He also began sending a stream of notes about what I should do after he died—things like canceling his magazine subscriptions so they didn't pile up and putting his house on the market in the spring, when the dogwoods would be in bloom. He even sent me the name of someone he wanted me to bar from attending his funeral, as they had had a recent falling-out.

I feared he was suicidal and felt responsible for saving him, the same way I felt as a child. One day I jumped into my car after twenty-four hours had gone by without his returning my messages (he wouldn't carry a cell phone or answer his home phone, but normally replied to emails within a few hours). I was so sure he had killed himself that I spent the entire drive to his house deciding whom to call first if I found him hanging from a closet or slumped dead in his reading chair. He finally called me as I was turning onto his street. He explained that he had lost electricity for a few hours, and, although he had gotten my phone messages, he hadn't returned them, as he needed to "burrow" for a while.

It would take three months of sessions with David for me to muster the courage to ask Dad to send his post-death instructions to his lawyer instead of me and to please seek professional help for his despair. I even played the what-Mom-would-want-for-you card, knowing she would want him to get help so he could once again enjoy life and be there for his family. Via email, he replied, *I hear you. I hear you. But there is nothing to be done.*

As we walked from the stadium parking lot to the entrance gate, I tried lightening the mood with some small talk—or, in this case, ball talk.

"So, what do you think about Manuel's decision to move Jimmy Rollins [the presumed lead-off hitter, who hadn't been hitting] to the number-seven spot in the lineup?"

"We'll see."

"Do you think we have enough pitching to win the NL East again?"

"We'll see."

As soon as we entered the ballpark, a ticket-taker handed Dad a Phillies Father's Day visor, which he promptly handed to me without saying a word.

When we arrived at our section, we were greeted by Tracy, the Phillies usher who had been wiping down our seats and checking our tickets for the past five seasons. She had heard about Mom's passing from Alan, who had attended a game with a buddy a few weeks earlier. I knew our fragile, this-is-just-another-father-daughter-outing illusion was in jeopardy when Tracy pulled my father's hand into her hands and said, "Martin, I am so sorry to hear about Wendy. She was such a great fan. I will miss having her in my section, and I know the Phillies will miss having her cheer them on."

Dad abruptly pulled his hand from her grasp, started tearing up, and swiftly climbed back up the steps toward the concourse, mumbling that he had to use the restroom. Tracy turned to me, her face as red as her Phillies cap, and apologized as if she had done something wrong, which I assured her she hadn't. It was still quite fresh for him, I said. Not to worry.

But as I slumped in my seat, I felt deeply worried. It was a mistake to have come here. How could we be doing something as ordinary as going to a baseball game when something so extraordinary had happened? How could I have put my father in this position? Suddenly, I felt more alone in that stadium of people than I had on any of my walks with Gracie. Surely no one in these stands had lost a mother or wife. How could they be cheering, eating—concerning themselves with Cole Hamels's lack of run support—if they had? How could they act so *normal*? This reminded me of my recent conversation with my hairdresser, Emily, who offhandedly asked if things were "back to normal." I took a breath and recalled she had not yet lost the mother she adored. If she had, she would have known that things would never be "back to normal." She would have known that "normal" was buried along with my mom, and that I couldn't yet imagine what a new normal might be. All I knew was that life without my mom felt horribly *abnormal*. But instead of actually saying this, I told her I was doing fine and asked if she could please not cut my bangs too short.

Dad returned from the bathroom in time for the National Anthem. Though neither of us said so, I knew we were both recalling how Mom used to relish singing the anthem along with the crowd. She was so proud of her US citizenship, so happy to be out with Dad, and so eager to cheer for her Fightin' Phillies that she sang with an unbridled enthusiasm that neither Dad nor I could match then, and certainly not now.

For a few innings, we found momentary relief in the rituals of fandom. Without having to think or speak, we were able to clap on cue as each Phillies player came to bat and each time our pitcher struck out a batter. And we naturally stood to applaud in the bottom of the second inning when our first baseman hit an RBI double. But when I turned to offer Dad a celebratory smile, he looked completely drained, as if he had run the bases himself.

I should just be glad he was going through the motions, I thought. At least he was here. At least he made the effort. Though we lived just eighteen miles apart, Dad consistently refused my invitations to come to my home for dinner, saying he was bad with directions. I offered to get him a GPS, but he refused that, too. His only presence in my house was the beautiful flower arrangement that he now sent every month.

He chose not to join my family for our Passover seder, saying he was going to take wine and matzo to Mom at the cemetery so she wouldn't be alone. When he emailed me his intention, I wanted to type back in big, bold letters, *Dad! If Mom exists in any way, shape, or form, she won't be at the cemetery on Passover; she will be at the Passover seder with all of us, which is exactly where she would want you to be, too!* But I just couldn't get the words out. I was still protecting him. And I understood from my own search for Mom how compelling it was to imagine her there.

During the third inning, I bought us each a hot dog and a Coke. It felt good to at least be able to offer him something he would accept. Then the gentleman who regularly sat in front of us turned to courteously ask how Mom was doing. Dad immediately jumped up from his seat and started making his way to the bathroom again—leaving me to tell this kind-faced fan that Mom had died. And when I did, I could tell I caught him off guard, so I quickly complimented him on how good he looked in his Father's Day visor and offered my dad's visor to his twelve-year-old son, who was sitting beside him.

I realized again, in the fourth inning of a Phillies game, that I had lost both parents—one to death and one to grief. It was as clear as the balls and strikes on the megawatt scoreboard. Even more gut-wrenching was acknowledging that while my father may have been a heroic figure to others while I was growing up (and I lauded him for that), he actually was never *my* hero—he never saved me from my own fears and aching loneliness. So why should I expect him to come through in the clutch for me now? In fact, wasn't it my dad who would tell anyone within earshot that I had been *his* rock this past year? Now I know how young men must feel when they learn all the statistics that weren't included on the back of their favorite players' baseball cards—like two stints in rehab, three failed marriages, and millions of dollars in debt.

The truth is, anyone I put up on a pedestal will eventually disappoint—be it Dad, David, or our MVP first-baseman, Ryan Howard. I felt bereft in an entirely new and profound way—mourning the fantasy father I never really had.

Normally my dad and I left during the seventh inning so we could avoid the traffic, but I knew that staying that long would be a stretch in more ways than one, so, since we had a three-run lead at the bottom of the fifth inning, I said we could go anytime he was ready. And without hesitation he said, "I'm ready now." And so was I. The juxtaposition of normal with abnormal had exhausted me.

The game wasn't over. But our day was.

WORLDS COLLIDE

It happened. The worst thing. The thing I dreaded. As Alan and I were opening our menus at our favorite sushi place, Naked Fish, I glanced up to see David walking into the restaurant with his wife and young daughter. He must have seen me first, as he offered a relaxed smile when our eyes met.

On the outside, I, too, looked relaxed and nodded politely, having rehearsed this moment in my mind hundreds of times before. Yet waves of nausea coursed through my body. If this were a scene in a disaster movie, it would be the moment when the bad guys break into the nuclear power plant and set off an alarm loud enough to alert all citizens to take immediate shelter—or else.

But this wasn't a movie. And there was no place to hide my alarm. So I burrowed my flushing cheeks inside the menu, hoping Alan wouldn't notice my mounting anguish.

Moments later, as the waiter served our spring rolls, David gave a quick wave toward Alan and me, reached for his daughter's hand, and left the restaurant. His wife, carrying their takeout order, followed closely behind.

I didn't cry until the next morning, when I called my friend Jane and told her what had happened the way one tells of being in a terrible car crash.

Jane: Hi there. Are you all right? I can't understand you, honey. Are you crying? Take a breath and tell me what's wrong.

Me: You'll never believe what happened.

Jane: Oh my God—what? Did someone die?

Me: No. But I wanted to. Last night Alan and I bumped into David and his family at Naked Fish.

Jane: You're kidding. Did he see you? What did you do?

Me: Yes, he saw me. And he waved. It was *awful*. He was holding his daughter's hand; she was wearing a pink Phillies cap. The three of them looked so perfect. It was a total nightmare.

Jane: Honey, I'm so sorry. It was bound to happen. You're okay. You'll be okay. Do you want me to come over? I can bring chocolate.

Me: No, thanks. I'm fine. I just can't stop crying. I'm never going to that restaurant again. Damn sushi.

Jane: Damn sushi!

Now I understand why eyewitness testimony is considered unreliable. For months I'd wondered what David's wife and daughter looked like; perhaps I'd already passed them in the grocery store or at the dry cleaner without knowing it. But if they were to walk into my house this very moment, I wouldn't recognize them—I had been too shocked to truly take in what they looked like. These were the people David belonged to and who belonged to him—the people who didn't have to pay for his time, hand, or love. Something inside me came undone. I could no longer deny their existence or the truth that he had a life beyond our weekly hour. It was one thing to know it intellectually, and another thing to see him and his family parading so happily together in front of me with their dumplings in tow. How dare they!

FINDING FRIEDA:

A DREAM REMEMBERED

It is a summer morning. I am walking along the Valley Green trail, the wooded path I traverse a few times a week. I am deep in thought, moving in the direction of Northwestern Avenue—back toward my car, toward my home. Suddenly I am swarmed from behind by a group of women on bikes. They are older women, perhaps in their late sixties or early seventies. All of them have strands of silver/gray hair sticking out of brightly colored helmets. And all of them are plump, if not actually *fat*. It is easy to notice their size because they are completely naked. Not even a thong in sight.

I am startled, as much by the ease with which they ride as by their nakedness. As the herd glides effortlessly past me, one rider turns back toward me. I want to look away so as not to embarrass her—or, more to the point, embarrass myself for being caught looking. But before I can, she flashes me a wide, knowing smile, as if she's been expecting to see me for quite a long time. Then she winks, turns back toward the front of her bike, and continues cycling.

As I reflected on the dream, my first thought was that these women represented my worst nightmare. They were everything I fear being: fat, old, naked, and exposed. Yet, much to my surprise, I couldn't deny how happy they were. They weren't racing to an artificial finish line. They weren't self-conscious. And they weren't alone. They were balanced comfortably on their bikes and in their own droopy, puffy, wrinkly skin. In fact, it would be fair to say they were more comfortable in their skin than I was in mine. And they were leading me toward home.

And it wasn't just one daring woman. They clearly drew strength and pleasure from being together, not as pioneers or rabble-rousers, not as streakers interrupting a ballgame or an awards ceremony, just a gaggle of women being wholly (and holy) in their individual and communal nature.

And it was then I realized that these women represented not just my fears but my wishes as well. They were exercising their freedom from the tyranny within. They were at ease—in flow— and they were beautiful.

I imagined a conversation between me and the woman who winked knowingly at me:

Me: Oh my goodness. How can you do this? Aren't you embarrassed?

Her: Embarrassed? Of what? My body? No way. Those days are over. This body has made it through a lot, and I'm darn proud of it. Three kids, two husbands, and at least twenty-two different diets at different times for different reasons—none of them, of course, delivering more than a moment's triumph. No, I'm not embarrassed. I'm free. Finally free.

Me: Wow. That is impressive. I mean startlingly impressive. I can't imagine.

Her: Well, honey, you did imagine. It's your dream, silly.

Me: Yes. I guess it is.

Her: Let me ask you, do you feel anything besides startled when you see us biking past you?

Me: I feel awe. Respect. Maybe a bit jealous. But then my incredulity comes back.

Her: Hmm. I get that. This is not only your dream but an image that seems beyond your dreams. Like, how could anyone, let alone an old woman, be this daring, this bold, this public in her nakedness?

Me: Yes, that's right. And as you say that, I also think it's interesting that you're riding on my path, the path that I diligently exercise on partly to ensure I don't ever look anything like you: fat and old and gray—no offense. But the irony is, I can't deny how happy you look, and beautiful. And you aren't alone. In fact, I was in the minority. I was alone on my walk, and you were with friends. Hmm.

Her: Indeed.

Me: Okay . . . so maybe it is possible to be happy, no matter what body I'm in. And maybe the path forward is about being naked, vulnerable. And just maybe vulnerability doesn't have to lead to death but can perhaps lead to liberation and intimacy. Yes! I think that's it. The more I am willing to risk, the closer I can get to home, *my* home, *my* essential self—to a connection within myself and among others. Pretty cool.

Her: I'll say!

Me: And I think the fact that you all were on bikes is significant as well. You weren't walking or running through the park. You were rolling along. Supported. You had help. It didn't look hard. And I'm finding that true for me, too—that life is so much better, and often easier with support, especially in the form of friends. Friends like Jane, Val, and Jean, who saved me from my hunger and let me dish about my therapist. I don't know where I'd be without them.

Her: You're right, Cheryl. At one time it was hard for me, but not now. Now, being with friends and feeling good in my own skin is as easy as riding a bike.

Me: Very funny. By the way, if you don't mind my asking, what's your name?

Her: Frieda. My name is Frieda.

Me: Well, thank you for your time, Frieda.

Frieda: Anytime, sweetie. Anytime.

GHOSTWRITER

Dear Cheryl,

Thank you for asking for my thoughts about being a first-time parent, which I am glad to share. I know it would be easier to continue idealizing me, or making excuses for my sometimes-poor parenting, but both of us realize that wouldn't contribute to your growth and healing.

As you know, I was twenty-two years old when you were born. I'm sure it's cliché to say I was still a child myself, but it was true. I had been in this country only eighteen months, and been married for less than a year, when you were born.

Being a new mom was overwhelming. Dad worked twelve-hour days, weekends, too, I didn't have a car, and my parents were still in South Africa. I had no experience caring for an infant. The neighbors helped a bit, but most of what I learned came by way of trial and error.

What I remember most about those early months was being absolutely terrified of breaking you.

Now, I see how that fear, combined with my homesickness and deep loneliness, led me to hold on too tight. You were just a baby, yet I treated you like my precious doll.

I suppose some children would push away from that kind of clinging—but not you. You were exquisitely sensitive, picked up on my neediness, and clung as tightly to me as I did to you. So tightly that even going to kindergarten became an unbearable severing for us both. I can still hear your wails as I ran out of the classroom—just as the teacher told me to do. What you didn't see was how I cried my own tears as soon as I reached the car, not knowing if I was crying for me or for you, perhaps for us both.

This daily drama was so wrenching that I was secretly relieved when the school principal suggested we take you out of kindergarten and try again the following year. It gave us more time together and more time to prepare for the inevitable separation.

And as for camp—well, it took more strength than I thought I had to read your letters, each one more desperate than the last. Pleading for us to take you home. Telling us you would be good, be better, do anything we asked, if we just let you come home. So many times I second-guessed our decision to send you away. I was torn between my heart, which wanted to rescue you, and my head, which said you had to learn how to be independent of me.

My sense now is that there was another way. And I should have worked harder to find it. I should have found a way to help you be successful in separating. I should have found more help for all of us. I was not very good at challenging authority—including your father—at that time in my life. And you paid for that.

Cheryl, I am so very sorry. And I know as I say that, you want to interrupt and tell me, "It's okay, Mom—you did your best. It's fine." But, honey, it's not okay. And it's not fine. I let you down. Big time. I know it. You know it. We can't change it, but we must acknowledge it.

I messed up a bit, Cheryl. I clung too tight. I used you to give me a sense of purpose and worth. Time and time again, I asked you to be a big girl, a good girl, a sweet girl, a pretty girl, never giving you space to be a real girl: a scared girl, a tough girl, an angry girl, a sad girl, or even a joyful girl. I just wanted you to be my girl. My Poppet. I didn't stand up to Dad and insist he get help. I didn't give you tools to help you make friends—I just kept throwing you into the deep end of the social waters and expecting you to swim effortlessly into your life.

But as I write, I see that's not all entirely true—and here comes the worst part. The deeper truth is, in my shadowy heart, I didn't want you to swim away. I wanted you to swim back to me. If I taught you how to make friends, you would leave me and I would be alone again.

There. I said the ugly nugget. The part I am most ashamed of. I let my need for security be more important than yours.

All the time, it looked to others like I was sheltering you, but really you were sheltering me. As long as you needed me, I had a noble role and a friend and an ally.

Gosh, it must have been incredibly confusing for you. One minute I was holding on tight, and the next I was pushing you out the door. And the worst part was, you believe the reason I sent you away was because you weren't a good enough daughter. No, Cheryl, it was because I wasn't a good enough mother then. Not nearly enough. And, it's not okay.

I all but sabotaged your noble attempts at independence. It was my fault you faltered and flailed, Cheryl. Never yours. Never.

I am sorry for how I misused you. I am sorry for my contribution to your wounding, and to the deep sense of unworthiness you have carried inside.

Now, before you tell me I'm being too hard on myself, let me say that sharing these truths is surprisingly liberating. I finally feel I'm doing right by you by saying how I did wrong. I know that may not make sense to you, but trust me, it's true.

So, if neither of us can change what happened forty-five years ago, why, then, am I making this confession now, especially when you have been so quick to defend me and to reassure me and David that you are fine? "It is what it is," you say.

But to gain the freedom and healing you are fighting for, you must acknowledge that you were wounded, that it hurt deeply, and that it was, in part, my actions and inactions, not yours, that caused such pain. Denial doesn't liberate, Cheryl. Speaking the truth does.

And the last bit of truth I have for today is this: You are my daughter and my friend. I am proud of you beyond measure. I will love you always.

Mom

This letter poured out of me one morning just as I had settled into my desk chair to attend to some paperwork. It was as if my mother were holding the pen herself.

OUT OF THE WOODS

AND INTO MY LIFE

I thought my most humiliating admission was telling David I wanted to run into the woods with him and make love for three days. It wasn't.

My most humiliating admission was sharing my stunning realization that even if David were in love with me (he wasn't), and even if he did run into the woods with me (he wouldn't) at some point, we would have to leave the woods. This came to me about a week after I ran into him at the sushi restaurant with his wife and daughter. Seeing him in such a mundane environment, dressed in shorts and a baseball cap and clearly happy to be with his family, made them painfully and undeniably real and jolted me from the fantasy island I had taken refuge on.

What have I been thinking? I asked myself, somewhat in horror. Clearly, I wasn't thinking at all. My rational mind had been hijacked by the primitive longings of my heart—facilitated in no small part by the amniotic cocoon that a good, and in this case good-looking, therapist like David provides.

"Oh my goodness," I breathlessly blurted to David at our next session, not even attempting to hide my chagrin. "I get it. I have been so focused on trying to be kind, pleasing, and pretty enough to get you to run into the woods with me, to have a healing love-fest on a blanket of pine needles, that I completely neglected to consider what would happen when we stepped out of the woods and back into our lives."

David smiled. "Well, that's the nature of fantasy, Cheryl. No reality allowed! That said, your question is a good one: What *do* you think would happen when we emerged from the woods?"

I paused.

"For starters, we would be exhausted from three days of passionate sex, and most likely covered in bug bites, possibly poison ivy, too. We'd have to go to our respective homes to shower and clean up. That part, I see. What I can't see is actually leaving Alan. Not now. Not after all we have invested in building our new family and in improving our marriage. He's been making unbelievable efforts to change and support me—telling me how beautiful I look every day, listening to me more deeply than I thought possible, and meditating daily to manage his stress. He's even walking Gracie! And despite the struggle, I still see his beautiful heart, the heart that moved me the night we first met. I see it and love him for it even more now. And despite all I've put him through this past year, he really does seem to love me.

"Plus, I can't see you giving up your practice, which you would have to do, not to mention leaving your own family to be with me. How could any good come from that? It wouldn't be healing; it would be horrible."

"All good points, Cheryl."

"And don't take this personally, but it did strike me that no matter what I think I feel for you, in reality, I know precious little about who you are and how you are when you're not being paid to listen to me. You could be a real pain in the ass for all I know."

I paused and looked David in the eyes (yes, in the eyes) to make sure I hadn't hurt his feelings. But I could tell by his grin I hadn't.

"I *can* be quite difficult to live with," he chuckled.

For an entire week, I basked in the relief of my newfound clarity. I felt as if I had dumped a two-hundred-pound ogre from my back. I finally got it—there was no "there" there. Even if I had David the way I thought I needed him, unless I changed my ways, the longing would come back, as always. It is all I have known, and all I thought I was worthy of having. Longing saved me when I was a child, but it was hurting me now. Longing is not living. Longing is not loving.

Longing had been my drug of choice. It was time to kick the habit once and for all.

Going cold turkey was easy at first. No shakes, no sweats, no pain. But ten days later, seemingly without warning, I came crashing down from my euphoric high. Alan was twenty minutes late for dinner and didn't call to let me know, my dad had sent a particularly despondent email, and my one-eyed, fifteen-year-old cat had just thrown up her medicine. I needed a fix. I longed to long. So I allowed myself just a small hit of fantasy and imagined showing up to our next session in a gauzy peach blouse, carrying a picnic basket and a bottle of wine. But this time, instead of my fantasy leading us straight to the woods, it led me straight to despair as I suddenly saw both of us becoming violently ill before we even had time to finish our first glass of wine or share a kiss.

"I feel more alone than ever," I cried to David the next time we met. "And sad. So very sad. I can't stop crying. It's like another death. My fantasies of us have become toxic. They used to feel so nourishing. They kept me company on my walks with Gracie; they comforted me when I struggled with Alan and soothed me when I missed my mom. Now every time I think of them, I immediately think of stepping out of the woods and into a disaster movie. It's like I've developed an allergy to my favorite food. It will never taste the same again. Damn it.

"Now what do I do?"

"You grieve."

"*What?* I came to therapy to lessen my grief, not to add to it. Can't you suggest something else?" I pleaded.

"You came to therapy to break free from some limiting patterns and beliefs. And you are. You are now strong enough to do the hardest part, Cheryl—to surrender one of the key strategies that saved you as a child. You are ready. You can do it. You *are* doing it. And it makes sense to me that it hurts like hell. You just crashed into your life. Your *real* life. You are like a newborn baby—an alien of sorts. You don't quite know where you are or what to do, but you will learn. If you stay close to your experience, you will learn."

I had never hated David more than I did at that moment.

But he was right. I did learn. And in the wake of my grief for the David I would never have and the David who most likely didn't even exist, I came to realize that my longing was both a healthy and human expression of life force *and* an overused strategy to avoid living and receiving in the present moment. I used longing, and the fantasies it fueled, as an escape from difficult, painful, messy situations and feelings, always believing that the answer to my pain was outside me—in this case, in the form of a man. And, to make matters worse, when I couldn't have that man, I believed it was proof of my unworthiness.

The truth is, in some ways I did go into the woods with David. I went deep into the forest of my psyche, and he accompanied me as a fearless and faithful sleuth and ally. And I *did* fall in love (or something like it) with him—in fact, I don't believe I could have survived my grief for my mother, my father, my childhood, my own child, and even the romantic illusions of marriage unless I had. Falling in love (or something like it) with David was my path in, but it wasn't my path out; it wasn't my panacea. The path out was forged when I began reconsidering my beliefs about why David wasn't running away with me, when I stopped working so hard to earn love, and when I found the courage to actually receive the love that was available.

And while I no longer lust for David, I do feel an immeasurable amount of affection and gratitude for him. And sometimes that affection and gratitude feels like love—but a wholesome love, not a lusty love. When I think of all he has done for me—tolerating, even *welcoming*, in equal measure my intense love and hate, and showing me seemingly unending curiosity, understanding, and equanimity—I feel totally gushy inside. But instead of allowing my gushiness to morph into fantasy, I am more likely to stay with it—to let the gushiness nourish me rather than diminish me.

And I no longer take his no-gifts and limited-self-disclosure policies personally, though they do still piss me off from time to time. And I occasionally imagine hanging one or two photographs on his waiting-room wall and have just the plant for his office if he ever changes his mind.

David asked me once what would be the worst part of not being in love with him. And I answered, "I'd have nothing." But the very next evening, I realized it was a lie. I was in my kitchen, nonchalantly emptying the dishwasher, when Andrew, just home from college, gave me a quick kiss on the cheek and offered to help. Then Becca ran into the kitchen, seeking my opinion on a new dress, and ten minutes later Alan walked in the front door, proclaiming, "The luckiest husband alive is home." Yes, I could no longer let longing eclipse the love that was available—scary, messy, imperfect, but available.

Finally, I was ready to exchange longing for belonging and truly receive the life I had built. The life my mother would have wanted for me.

STRIKE UP THE BAND

Three months after the baseball game, I had lunch with my
father and he sent me home with a dozen oatmeal-raisin
cookies, three novels for Alan, and a three-by-three-inch box
holding an eight-millimeter tape. The tape was dated June 17,
1964, two days after I was born. He said he had found it when
cleaning out a closet. He didn't know what was on the tape but
thought it might interest me.

I promptly had the tape converted to a CD. Then I placed it
atop my to-be-read pile on a red wooden end table that sits beside my desk. Curious but also cautious, I spent weeks casually
glancing at the CD—noticing the date stenciled neatly in black
and white. I expected it to be a recording my mom made for her
parents back in South Africa soon after I was born.

I readied myself to play the CD on the Jewish holy day of
Yom Kippur, often referred to as the Day of Atonement, when
Jews ask for forgiveness of their sins so they may be inscribed
in the Book of Life the following year. It is the holiest day of
the Jewish year. My mother cherished this day and the rituals of
prayer, fasting, and quiet reflection that went along with it. Since

I was especially homesick for her, I decided it was a good day to play the CD and resurrect her twenty-two-year-old voice.

I loaded the CD into my laptop and pressed PLAY. To my surprise, the first voice I heard was my grandfather's: "This is Cheryl Lee's birthday tape. It is recorded on the seventeenth of June, 1964, as Granny and I wait for our telephone call to be put through so we can congratulate her, her parents, and her grandparents the Rices on her arrival on the fifteenth."

Tears immediately spilled from my eyes. It had been almost thirteen years since I had heard my beloved grandfather's slightly mischievous voice, and even more years since I'd heard my granny speak.

For nearly ten minutes, there was anxious conversation between my grandparents and the overseas operator, all of them trying to find the correct phone number and the right hospital, then convincing the right person at the hospital to put the call through, despite its being past visiting hours. Finally, the information was gathered and the call was transferred.

The relief in my mother's voice when she heard her parents on the phone was palpable. She wearily but proudly proclaimed me a healthy, beautiful, six-pound baby girl who resembled her sister, Sandy. Hearing this, my grandfather began to weep.

My grandparents spoke briefly to my father, who was holding and feeding me at the time. My grandfather encouraged him to make sure Mom didn't do too much when she returned home. Then, just a few minutes later, they promised to speak again soon, shared tearful "I love yous," and hung up. But the celebration continued. The next hour of the recording consisted of congratulatory messages from twenty-five of my grandparents' close friends and relatives who had gathered in their home to celebrate my arrival.

I could hear, one by one, my grandfather greeting each visitor at the door: "Clara, come here and record your well wishes for Wendy and Martin and their baby girl, Cheryl." Then each guest exuberantly shared his or her good wishes: "Mazel tov, Wendy and Martin." "Welcome to the world, little Cheryl. Bunny and I are overjoyed at your arrival." "Knowing Wendy, I'm sure she's a beautiful baby." "Health and happiness to all of you." After about eight or nine friends had spoken, my great-uncle secured the microphone and urged all the revelers to raise their glasses and toast my parents and me. Then he led the group in a South African rendition of "For She's a Jolly Good Fellow."

Hearing the rejoicing my entrance into the world had prompted was startling. A party. Tears of joy. Wine and song. What was next, I wondered—a marching band parading through their living room? This was quite possibly the biggest and only bicontinental birthday celebration I had ever had. And I didn't even know about it until forty-six years after it happened.

Never before had I known a time when I, Cheryl Lee Rice, lived in the world with no confessions to make, nothing to atone for. Atoning for my limitations and foibles was not something I did only on Yom Kippur. My birthday, the first day of the year, even the start of school in September were occasions to take stock, make amends, and set new goals for being a better, more worthy version of myself.

But now I was being introduced to a moment when, cradled tenderly in my father's arms, I was beautiful, wanted, and whole. How astonishing to hear myself being welcomed into the world with merriment and song. What I had spent my entire life doubting—namely, my inherent worthiness—was now turned upside down as the undeniable evidence was played back to me on tape.

Oh, what delight in finally meeting the me who has been here all along—my essential, irrefutable, wholly lovable self. No apology necessary.

So bring on that marching band.

I MARRIED THE GREEN LANTERN

One afternoon a few months after we bought our king-size mattress, Alan called me from his office and said, "Honey, I have a surprise for you."

"What is it?"

"Well, I can't tell you, but I'll show you tonight."

"Okay. Do I have to dress up for it?"

"Nope. I'll be home by seven."

I thought perhaps he had bought tickets to a play he knew I wanted to see, or had landed a new client.

I wasn't even close.

Gracie saw him first. She usually barks in high-pitched, giddy anticipation when she sees Alan's car pull up, but now her bark was low and defensive. I stood up and went to the door. When I opened it, I almost started barking that way, too.

Alan was dressed head to toe in a green bodysuit and mask. I prayed this wasn't an inspired invitation for kinky sex. Things were better between us, but not that much better!

With curious astonishment, I said, "Oh my goodness. Who have we here?"

As if on cue, he replied, *"In brightest day, in blackest night, no evil shall escape my sight. Let those who worship evil's might beware my power. . .*

"I'm the Green Lantern, honey. That's my oath. What's for dinner?"

Fortunately, once Gracie heard Alan speak, she replaced her defensive bark with her happy-to-see-her-daddy squeal.

Over dinner Alan told me that one of his clients, the CEO of a charter school, had honored him and a few of his colleagues during the opening ceremony for the new school building Alan had helped them finance. During the ceremony, the CEO likened Alan to a superhero—the Green Lantern, to be specific—for the herculean efforts he'd put forth to bring the project to fruition, and gave him a Green Lantern bodysuit and mask. Alan had adored working with the CEO and her staff and was tickled by the acknowledgment—so much so that he decided to dress up as the Green Lantern not just for me, but also for the school's kindergarten students, whom he had read to that afternoon.

It was impossible not to be touched by his desire to share his generous playfulness with me. Alan had put on a mask to call forth his natural tenderness, and I had taken mine off and was ready to receive it. While we ate our dessert, I couldn't help smiling at the irony: just when I had surrendered my fantasy of a rescuing prince, in walked a superhero.

DEAR MOM

I just said good night to Mark, Jamie, Ben, and Rachel. Jamie is doing great. She finished treatment, her hair has grown back curly, and, most important, her cancer is in remission. What a blessing. You wouldn't believe how tall Ben is! He'll be starting tenth grade this year and is already talking about college. And Rachel, now an official tween at the ripe age of eleven, is wild about ballet and still wields a smile and vocabulary as big as Texas. Mark and Jamie both looked wonderful, especially considering they had just driven ten hours to get here. They are visiting for the week and Alan and I hosted a welcome dinner in their honor.

Alan's dad came, as did Aunt Sandy and Uncle Bart. Aunt Sandy has become such a dear and important person to me, not just because being with her makes me feel closer to you, but because of her own remarkable strengths, stories, and wisdom. She's even picked up where you left off by letting me know when she thinks my hair is too long. And she's been an amazing champion of my writing. I am so grateful. I know you would be overjoyed by that. Of course

Andrew and Becca were here, too, and helped prepare the food without my having to ask. They seem to relish their status as the older cousins to Ben and Rachel, who eagerly seek them out.

I'm sure you're wondering if Dad came. Well, not only did he join us, but he actually drove here on his own for the first time, which tells you a bit about how he's doing. He's doing okay, Mom. Better. As he would say, he's trying. And I know you would be proud of him for that. Sometimes, though, I feel overwhelmed by his grief and my helplessness to heal him. But I'm sure you would tell me it is not my responsibility to heal Dad. It never was. I must let him grieve in his own way and trust that he will come through this in time. I can't make Dad's anguish my own.

On nights like this, I miss you fiercely. Tonight, when everyone was sitting in the sunroom, kibitzing and eating dessert (yes, dark chocolate was included!), I couldn't help but imagine you here, too. You would have effortlessly yet purposely been touching and chatting with each and every person, gushing about how pretty the house looked and organizing the week's activities. And while I'm truly sorry you weren't with us, missing you didn't stop me from feeling the joy of this evening myself. I even ate a whole piece of cheesecake, did a pirouette with Rachel, and left the dishes in the sink for Alan to wash. I felt relaxed and full in ways I never thought possible in the wake of your death.

After you died, I was lost beyond words, beyond reason, it seemed. I ached to reach out to Kelly for comfort, but I soon realized that the Kelly I wanted was as gone to me as you are. Still, I kept looking for you everywhere I went in the world. I even went to our old home on Highland Drive (but please don't ask for the details, as that didn't turn out so great). It took a while to discover the truth—you are completely and forever gone, and you are also completely and forever alive within me. I can't believe I just wrote that. It has taken me three years of grieving, searching, longing, stumbling, crying, doubting, raging, and reconciling to understand this. I suppose it is the kind of truth that can be found only through a journey like the one I've been on. It isn't something I could have read in a condolence card—and even if I had, I wouldn't have believed it.

Perhaps in the most important ways, you never left. Perhaps you have been with me all along, holding my hand throughout this process. Not as a bird, or a message on a billboard, or a white-winged angel, but as a whole and holy source of strength and comfort inside me. Once upon a time, you sheltered me for nine months inside the womb of your body, and now, for the rest of my life, I will hold you inside the womb of my heart. I am reminded of a quote by the poet I used to tell you about, John O'Donohue: "Often it seems that we have to undertake the longest journey to arrive at what has been nearest all along."

Mom, I can't deny how much I miss picking out paint colors with you, feasting on your brisket, and talking with you on the phone each week. Yet lately I am starting to trust my own decorating and culinary inclinations. For instance, Alan assures me that the emerald-green tile in the bathroom looks just right and keeps asking for my turkey chili, even when it's hot outside! And now that I know where you are, inside me, we can talk all I'd like. I could have sworn I heard you laughing when I told you just yesterday how Gracie ate an entire piece of bubble gum—including the wrapper!

But guess what? Yours isn't the only voice I reach for when I need comfort, encouragement, wisdom; I'm coming to seek and hear the sound of my voice, too. At first it was quite fuzzy and nondescript, like an unfamiliar flavor in a big bowl of soup. But the more I paid attention, with curiosity and self-compassion, the more distinct—and, dare I say, flavorful—my voice became. In fact, it's not uncommon for me to actually put my hand to my cheek or on my heart and whisper kind words to myself if I've had a particularly hard day. "Hey there, sweetie. I'm here. You're not alone. I know your heart. You just feel what you need to feel. You're okay. I love you." Day by day, I am becoming more like myself, and day by day, I am liking myself more. What a revelation that is.

And I have David to thank for that. Yes, I'm still seeing him, though we have cut back on our sessions. I remember just after you died, when I was sick with sorrow, David suggested we meet twice a week for a while. At first I balked— "I'm not suicidal!" I insisted. But then I realized it wasn't because I wanted to die that he suggested we meet more often; it was because he sensed how much I wanted to live. And he was right, Mom. I want to live—freely, purposefully, and courageously. Not just to please you or to honor your memory—but to please me and honor the life I have. And David has been instrumental in helping me do so. I have enormous appreciation for all he has done for me. And you'll be glad to know I see him as a masterful therapist and nothing more. Yes, in the beginning I wanted to be with him passionately and desperately, but in the end I found myself and real passion—real love with Alan.

Speaking of Alan, he was his charming, gregarious self at dinner tonight. You were always so touched by his charm and often told me, "That man loves you, Cheryl." You were right. I'm thankful that despite all I've put him through, he still loves me. And I love him. And we are going to therapy, taking long weekends together without the kids, and supporting each other's professional ambitions without reservation.

It's funny that we mark the growth of our children by recording their heights on bedroom doorjambs and gasping at how tall they have grown upon their return from summer camp. But it's harder to tell when adults grow. I figure I should be at least two and a half inches taller to accommodate all I have learned these past few years!

And part of the growth comes from letting go. Letting go of my remorse for not having had a child of my own; letting go of the grief and hunger games I played after you died; letting go of the notion that love must be earned, and that it's my job to heal people, including Dad. In fact, though I still have tremendous compassion for all the suffering he has endured and also tremendous respect for the way he gives to others despite his suffering, I am getting better at making requests of him and tolerating his discomfort at social gatherings. Mostly I enjoy the father he is and have let go of the daddy he couldn't be. I really do know that he did the best he could. As did you. As did all of us, Mom.

A friend recently shared her belief that people unconsciously choose when to be born and when to die. At first I doubted this. Now I see that if you hadn't died when you did, *consciously or not, I wouldn't have started on this journey at this point in my life—a journey that begins and ends with me. What a tragedy it would be if, at eighty years of age, I still hadn't found this path to me.*

Gracie just curled up in her bed. She is exhausted from hosting a houseful of guests and scanning the carpets for crumbs. I can tell by her sighs that she is glad they are gone—the guests, not the crumbs!

I'm pretty tired myself. It was a big night. I'm glad to be home. In fact, grieving your loss revealed to me that I didn't just feel homesick at summer camp; I was homesick all my life—mostly for a relationship with myself that is healthy, nurturing, and abiding. It is the foundation that makes all other relationships—mutual and meaningful relationships—possible. I see that now. And I have that now, Mom. I'm not homesick anymore.

Love always,
Cheryl

ACKNOWLEDGMENTS

Thank you to Janet Falon for tenderly receiving and critiquing my first post-Mom essays.

Jennifer Schelter, much gratitude for welcoming me into a community where I could write freely for the first time.

Dad, you gave me the best gift a budding memoirist could ask for when you looked me in the eyes and said, "Cheryl, you have to write your truth. You will cheat yourself if you don't." Thank you, Dad. I love you.

To Jane Weiss, Jean Hurd, and Valerie Root Wolpe: together and separately, you have kept me faithful to my path, fortified me with your belief in the worth of my words, and, when necessary, threatened me with bodily harm if I even considered abandoning my goal. Thank you, dear ones.

To my dedicated cheerleaders Sandy Silverman, Mark Rice, Kristen Craft, Lisa Gallagher, Leslie Mayer, Nedra Fetterman, and Pat Shannon: each of you honored me with your unwavering interest in and energy for my writing, helped me be brave, and on more than one occasion made me laugh.

Hilary Illick and Lorraine Marino, you were not just trusted first readers but have also been trusted friends, role models, and sages. Thank you for holding this book, and my purpose in writing it, with both hands and full hearts.

To my therapist: You came in when it seemed the rest of the world had gone out. Thank you for your fierce commitment to my freedom and wholeness, and for being there no matter how deep, dark, thick, or scary the territory. You welcomed it all. You welcomed me.

Anne Dubuisson, I couldn't have asked for a better editorial guide than you. Thank you for holding the vision of this book from the moment we met, for believing in my ability to bring that vision to life, and for being an absolute delight to work with.

And to my sweet, sexy husband, Alan Wohlstetter, your steadfast support and encouragement for my growth as a writer and a woman have been life-altering. Thank you for showing me every day the truth in true love.

ABOUT THE AUTHOR

Cheryl Rice is a professional speaker and coach. Her company, Your Voice Your Vision, partners with women striving to be leaders in their own lives. When Cheryl decided to take the advice she so passionately offers her clients, she emerged with a memoir. Her essays have appeared in The Philadelphia Inquirer, Cactus Heart, and Cure Magazine. Cheryl has M.S. degrees in both Psychological Services and Organi-zation Development, and lives with her family outside of Philadelphia. Find Cheryl and a free downloadable reader's guide online at www. YourVoiceYourVision.com.

Selected Titles From She Writes Press

She Writes Press is an independent publishing company founded to serve women writers everywhere. Visit us at www.shewritespress.com.

Her Beautiful Brain: A Memoir by Ann Hedreen. $16.95, 978-1-938314-92-6. The heartbreaking story of a daughter's experiences as her beautiful, brainy mother begins to lose her mind to an unforgiving disease: Alzheimer's.

Splitting the Difference: A Heart-Shaped Memoir by Tré Miller-Rodríguez. $19.95, 978-1-938314-20-9. When 34-year-old Tré Miller-Rodríguez's husband dies suddenly from a heart attack, her grief sends her on an unexpected journey that culminates in a reunion with the biological daughter she gave up at 18.

Warrior Mother: A Memoir of Fierce Love, Unbearable Loss, and Rituals that Heal by Sheila K. Collins, PhD. $16.95, 978-1-938314-46-9. The story of the lengths one mother goes to when two of her three adult children are diagnosed with potentially terminal diseases.

Pregnant Pause: A Memoir of Acceptance by Colleen Haggerty. $16.95, 978-1-63152-923-8. Haggerty's candid story of how she overcame the pain of losing a leg at seventeen—and of terminating two pregnancies as a young woman—and went on to become a mother, despite her fears.

Four Funerals and a Wedding: Resilience in a Time of Grief by Jill Smolowe. $16.95, 978-1-938314-72-8. When journalist Jill Smolowe lost four family members in less than two years, she turned to modern bereavement research for answers—and made some surprising discoveries.

Think Better. Live Better. 5 Steps to Create the Life You Deserve by Francine Huss. $16.95, 978-1-938314-66-7. With the help of this guide, readers will learn to cultivate more creative thoughts, realign their mindset, and gain a new perspective on life.

www.ingramcontent.com/pod-product-compliance
Lightning Source LLC
LaVergne TN
LVHW050853100625
813472LV00005B/626